KT-074-936

THE HISTORY OF THE NUDE IN PHOTOGRAPHY

written by
PETER LACEY
designed by
ANTHONY LaROTONDA

A GALLERY EDITION BANTAM BOOKS NEW YORK

THE HISTORY
OF THE NUDE IN
PHOTOGRAPHY/
A Bantam Gallery
edition/published
April 1964.
Library of Congress
Catalog Card Number:
63-14181. All rights
reserved. Copyright
© 1964, by Bantam
Books, Inc. Published
simultaneously in the
United States and
Canada. Bantam Books
are published by
Bantam Books, Inc. Its
trade-mark, consisting
of the words "Bantam
Books" and the
portrayal of a bantam,
is registered in the
United States Patent
Office and in other
countries. Marca
Registrada. Printed in
the United States
of America.
Bantam Books, Inc.,
271 Madison Ave.
New York 16, N. Y.

PHOTO CREDITS:
Culver Pictures, N. Y.
pp 9, 10, 13, 15.
Galaxy Photos pp 16, 19.
George Eastman House,
Rochester pp 25, 28-31.
Metropolitan Museum
of Art, N. Y. pp 40-43.
Library of Congress,
Washington, D. C.
pp 45, 48-53.
Magnum Photos, N. Y.
pp 73, 76-85.
Rapho-Guillumette
Pictures, N. Y.
pp 99, 102-107, 177,
180-189.

contents

The female nude—magical, erotic, aesthetic—has been modeled and painted since prehistory. Appearing rarely and awkwardly in the earliest art, she attained fulfillment and glory in ancient Greece. In their idealized treatment of the nude, the Greeks established a standard that only the asceticism of the Middle Ages ignored. The artists of the Renaissance and their successors of the eighteenth and nineteenth centuries revived the nude, and by the 1830's she was again a conventional form. It was inevitable that she should become a favorite subject of photography.

Today, photographs of the nude are so commonly published and seen that we hardly notice individual pictures unless they are particularly shocking, or are of a famous actress, or (best of all) both. Reputable advertisers and mass magazines increasingly use nude photographs of varying quality to attract and interest the purchasing public. Disregarding the ageless glut of pornography, the photographed female nude is more evident and acceptable now than ever before in her hundred-year history. In America there are still

introduction

a few general publishing restrictions and many local laws of varying strength and sanity. Nevertheless, we have come a long way from the innocent Victorian days when many shocked citizens were certain that no honest woman would willingly pose in front of a camera without her clothes on (and, therefore, that those models who were not prostitutes were undoubtedly the pathetic wives and sisters of the photographers, dragooned unwillingly and protestingly). Today, most of us are too sophisticated to believe this, but, nevertheless, the nude as a legitimate and serious subject of photography is still regarded with suspicion.

There are a number of reasons for this suspicion. One of them is that the vast majority of the photographs seen by the public have no aesthetic merit whatever. The pin-up is the most widely seen photographic nude, and the six pictures included in this Introduction are fair examples of this type produced over the last seventy-five years. Editors still look for the "sexy" (not sexual) nude. Occasionally, usually in the photographic annuals published here and abroad, a group of excellent pictures may appear. Generally, however, the nude photographs printed are either pictorially sexy or merely ineffectually arty. This situation is closely related to another cause of suspicion: our social and moral attitudes toward nudity itself. It is not the intention of this book to examine the reasons for these attitudes; even where explicable, they are not readily correctible. Thousands of specious (though sincere) words have been written about the nude and "pure" form in both art and photography. Sir Kenneth Clark, an eminent art historian who has not side-stepped the issue, has pointed out that the erotic is, and must always be, present in the nude. It must be accepted that the erotic is not necessarily the pornographic. There is, finally, a third and perhaps most important reason for the suspicion of the photographed nude that does seem correctible: the belief that photography cannot quite attain the level of fine art and that this somehow lessens the value of even the finest photographs.

The question of the artistic status of photography has been continually discussed since the very invention of the camera. Those who do not believe it is an art point to the seemingly accidental nature of the process (the photographer has no real control over his medium to the degree that the artist has) and the fact that the photograph is always a picture of a particular or real thing, whereas a painting or drawing is a generalization, an interpretation. This specific quality of the camera is never more apparent than in a photograph of a nude: we are looking at an individual, real woman. However, we will always misunderstand and under-appreciate the finest photography if we insist on judging it by the standards of fine art. What we must look for are photographs which combine the camera's unique qualities with a sense of form and mood. The fine pictures in this volume exhibit the photographic qualities of accident (intentionally caught), individuality, immediacy. They are, we believe, worthy of the same consideration we traditionally give to works of art.

These photographs have a secondary value which becomes apparent in their roughly chronological arrangement: they demonstrate the imaginative ways in which several generations of photographers have explored the potentialities of their medium through the recurring use of one form. The history of the nude in photography is the history of the developed styles of a relatively small number of imaginative photographers. For this reason, the arrangement of this book is a series of portfolios of their characteristic work.

The connections and affinities between contemporary artists and photographers have frequently been close over the last century, but never more so than at the very beginning of photography. The nineteenth-century painters of France were among the first to study closely and copy photographs of the nude. Nude models were among the first subjects observed by the infant camera. According to Gernsheim, the French photographer Lerebours photographed some nudes as early as 1840, only one year after the historic introduction of Daguerre's process.

The popularity of the nude at this period was not only aesthetic: the professional models were among the few live subjects capable of holding a pose for the required five to ten minutes. The innovation of faster photographic techniques did not, however, lessen their popularity. Such artists as Ingres, Courbet, and Delacroix were quick to appreciate the value of the photographed nude. Poses ordered (and often directed) by them were done regularly by such early Parisian photographers as Nadar and Durieu. The camera could capture poses too difficult for the model to hold for long, and a series of different poses could reveal unexpected possibilities. In addition, model fees could be minimized. The models themselves, who were often prostitutes, found that an artfully posed figure study was an enticing form of advertising, a realization that has endured in modified form to this day.

In Victorian England the bond between photography and art was not so close or fruitful as in France. In London there was no close coterie of photogra-

phers and painters comparable to that in Paris; creative photography was done largely by the independent amateur. Moreover, photographers in England made the mistake of attempting to emulate painting. The few nudes visible in Victorian photographs are usually languid participants in banal, morally edifying allegorical arrangements. These photographs only emphasize the worst aspects of the paintings they strove to resemble. All in all, the nude found nineteenth-century England a chilly climate.

Even the insipid nudes of the Victorian pictorialist photographers got into trouble with the staid Photographic Society of London, to say nothing of the English Society for the Suppression of Vice, which led the defenders of purity in the 1850's. In France the situation was almost as bad. The middle-class furor over the realistic nude paintings of Manet and Courbet extended to the graphic realism of the camera: there was something *too* nude about a photographed nude. Under these circumstances the nude temporarily abandoned realism for the protective cloud of impressionism. In the latter half of the nineteenth century, photographers began to envelop her in a haze of blurred focus and dense shadow. But as the fog lowered, out of it came a series of striking nudes by a photographer-scientist with a non-aesthetic purpose: the study of human locomotion.

In the 1880's, academic painters in Europe and America were intrigued by the action photos of Eadweard Muybridge, an Englishman working in America. Their appeal was perfectly understandable: the meticulously literal style of the popular art of the period demanded visual "veracity." The motion studies of Muybridge solved many technical painting problems and showed new possibilities. Today, most of the paintings of the school repose in museum attics, but Muybridge's photographs are displayed and continue to interest us. Muybridge's work particularly interested the distinguished American painter Thomas Eakins. Eakins himself made some motion pictures with his own technique, but his most memorable photographs are his posed nudes. They have a

photographic simplicity unusual for the period.

Meanwhile, the majority of art-conscious photographers in America and abroad continued to clothe the nude in a fashionable (and morally necessary) haziness. A popular sub-style was the pseudo-classical vein with emphasis on billowing drapery as in the Charles Schenk DRAPERIES IN ACTION series of the 1890's. However, Schenk in his naïveté was hopelessly out of the mainstream of "creative" photography. In 1886, the English photographer Peter Henry Emerson had sounded the clarion call that was to unite art and science in "naturalistic" photography. This approach to photography reached its culmination in the work of a group calling themselves the "Photo-Secessionists," led by Alfred Stieglitz in the first two decades of this century.

The Photo-Secessionists were intensely concerned with the public acceptance of photography as an art. Their photographs, lavishly reproduced in their magazine CAMERA WORK, sought very often to capture the quality of the turn-of-the-century academic print or drawing. Almost any kind of manipulation, photographic or otherwise, was permissible as long as the desired result was obtained. The nudes produced by these photographers are most memorable when mood and photographic quality overcome or balance pretentious texture and lighting. Essentially, though, this path led to a dead end and it was Stieglitz himself who rescued the nude from artistic shadows.

The later nudes of Alfred Stieglitz and those of Edward Weston mark the decisive turning point in the history of the nude in photography. No longer interested in proving artistic points, they explored the camera on its own terms. The *photographic* nude was consistently seen for the first time. Beyond Stieglitz and Weston the history of the photographic nude becomes contemporary in the sense that all subsequent work of significance is *photographic* in intent and execution. It is by their individual styles that the later photographers have distinguished their work. In that work the nude continues to reveal her seemingly inexhaustible possibilities: the softly focused elegance of Arnold Genthe's dancers; the linear clarity of Harry Callahan's compositions with their sure command of the power of black and white; the restless experimentation of Ferenc Berko and Charles Swedlund; the sensitive reportage of Marvin Newman, Frank Horvat and René Groebli; the romantic visions of Emmanuel Sougez and J. Frederick Smith; the formally posed figures of Ruth Bernhard and Robert Wilson; the dynamic forms of Lucien Clergue; the uniquely photographic approach of Bill Brandt with his brilliant distortion of conventional forms.

Though the number of significant photographers of the nude is relatively small, it must be emphasized that this volume does not include all of them. There are a few notable omissions who, for one reason or another, could not be included. Yet this collection is as complete and representative as the editor could make it. It by no means attempts to be a definitive history of the nude in photography but, rather, a survey of the best work done since the invention of the camera. It is hoped that these pictures will reveal the great diversity of photographic approaches to the subject of the nude.

Not only are photographers as a group more concerned with the expression of form and style through the nude than painters and sculptors today, but, it can be argued, photography is at present the last refuge of the nude. Today in art the nude, if she appears at all, is simply one more form among others. The expression of her moods and nuances, as well as her actual form, have been abandoned to the realism of photography. Yet the photographic nude is not simply the literally realistic nude that the progressive nineteenth-century painters abandoned. In the work of the best photographers the beauty and meaning of the nude are shown with a graphic directness unique to the camera. In their photographs the nude has been seen in ways never conceived before. However, despite this situation, the photographers and painters occasionally continue to inspire or echo each other, as the reader will undoubtedly discover here.

—Peter Lacey

EUGÈNE DELACROIX
and
EUGÈNE DURIEU

The painter Eugène Delacroix (1798-1863) was particularly interested in photography and loved to study photographs of the nude, from which he learned "far more by looking than the inventions of any scribbler could teach me" (Journal, October 5, 1855). Like other artists, Delacroix also began to send models to pose for photographs from which he could make drawings and studies for paintings. Among the photographers who did such work for Delacroix was Eugène Durieu. A president of the Société Francaise de Photographie, Durieu was active in Paris in the 1850's. An advocate of "straight" photography, he was prominent in denouncing the then popular habit of heavily retouching photographs in an effort to render them more artistic.

An album of Durieu's photographs is in the possession of the George Eastman House in Rochester, New York, and among the pictures are a number of nudes. Beaumont Newhall has pointed out ("Delacroix and Photography," Magazine of Art, November 1952) that these nudes correspond to a description of an album of models that Delacroix's friend Constant Dutilleux owned. Dutilleux claimed that the models in his album had been posed by Delacroix. The artist himself mentions Durieu in several entries in his journal: on June 18th, 1854, Delacroix spent the whole day in Durieu's studio posing models. The Eastman House nudes also are reminiscent of the painter's style.

The nudes themselves, aside from their interest as art history, seem as placidly alive today as they were in front of the camera over a century ago. The poses are just that: poses. The camera seems to have been anchored to a spot before which the models were arranged, usually at the same distance. The fact that the picture-taking process was technically formidable does not entirely explain the quality of these nudes. They were consciously posed to resemble contemporary paintings and, in the absence of any evidence to the contrary, we can assume that Durieu regarded this as the proper way to approach the subject of the nude. The nude could be made socially and aesthetically acceptable by association with academic fine art. Art, at this time, found the nude acceptable only when subdued by a romantic, sentimental, or exotic context; the realistic nude was another matter, as Manet was to find. The Durieu nudes are a curious blend of romanticism and realism in that the poses are academic but the models are quite real in their individuality. The truce between the camera and "art" was an uneasy one and would not long endure.

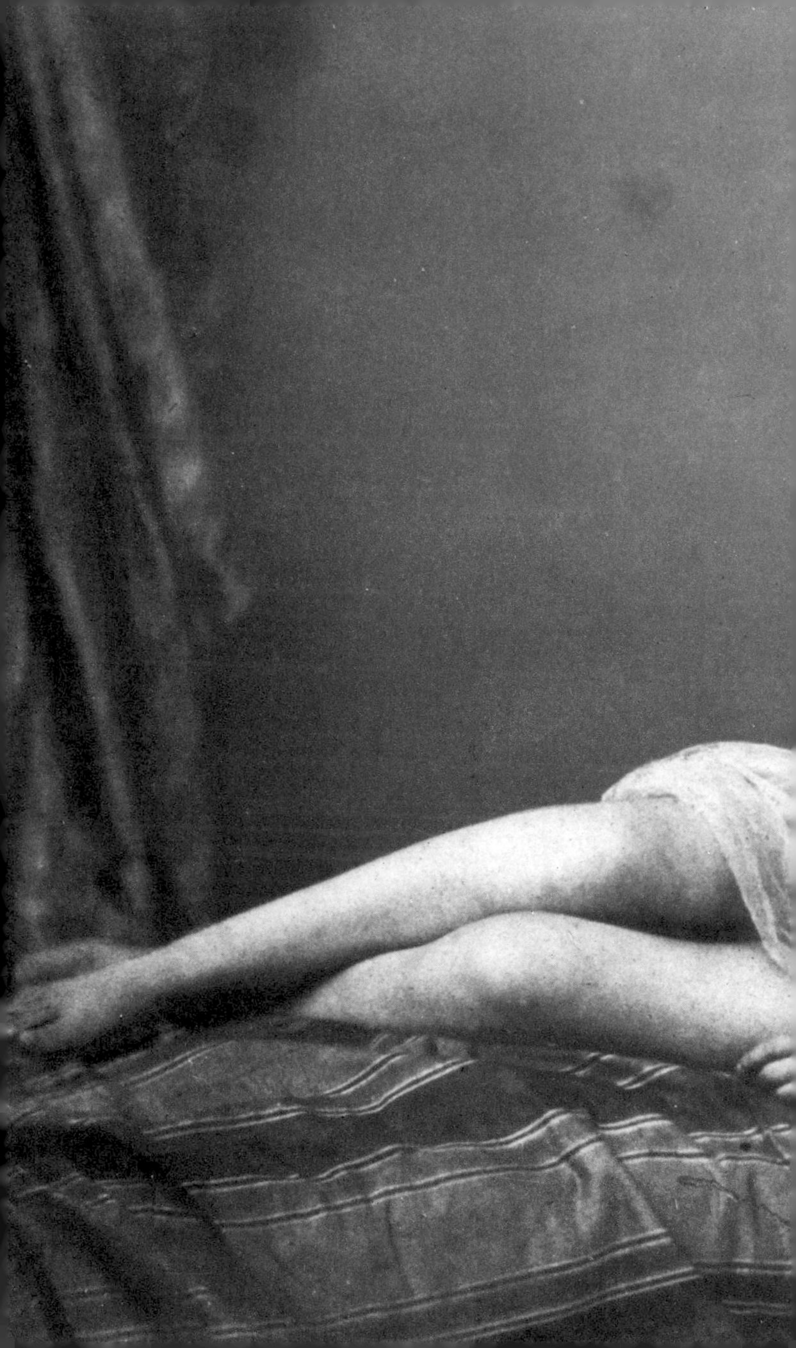

EADWEARD MUYBRIDGE and THOMAS EAKINS

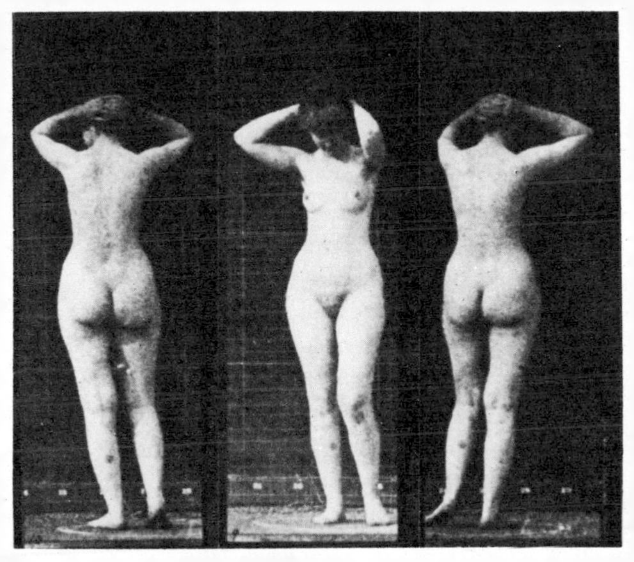

Most of Eadweard Muybridge's studies of "human locomotion" were done at, and under the auspices of, the University of Pennsylvania Academy of Art in Philadelphia during the years 1883-1884. Thomas Eakins, the foremost American painter of the period, had been instrumental in bringing the English photographer from California, where he had attracted attention with his action photographs of running horses. Eakins, a photographer himself, had been intrigued by Muybridge's technique. As director of the Academy, he used his influence to secure Muybridge's appointment.

At Philadelphia Muybridge expanded his study to include humans as well as many kinds of animals and birds. The technique used to capture the movement sequences essentially consisted of a number of cameras placed at regular intervals along a track running before a dark backdrop. The models simply moved along the track in various ways. As they performed, automatically timed shutters enabled the cameras to photograph their movements at regular intervals. In this way almost 100,000 negatives were exposed. The pictures have a kind of vitality that does not diminish with age. This vitality is probably due to two things: the obvious individuality of the models and the movement implied by *the photographic sequences.*

While Muybridge was experimenting with his multiple-camera technique, Eakins observed his methods closely. Eakins decided that a single camera with a revolving negative would be more satisfactory and succeeded in developing one. Unfortunately, he did not pursue this interest and few of his action sequences exist. His most significant photographs are single pictures and among them are a number of female nudes. Eakins was fascinated by the nude. The two nudes illustrated here (pages 40-43) are probably of artists' models at the Academy. Their poses are straightforward and honest, as were Eakins' paintings. Such honesty was not tolerated in Philadelphia in the '80's, and Eakins was often in conflict with the governors of the Academy. Eventually a furor arose over his uninhibited use of nude models in his art classes and he was forced to resign. Today, his nudes, both painted and photographed, are accepted and admired; his teaching methods are a matter of course in many art schools. What makes his photographs of the nude especially notable for their period is Eakins's disregard (in these particular pictures) for any of the exotic, sentimental, or moralizing overtones that seem to have been a necessary ingredient of the Victorian nude.

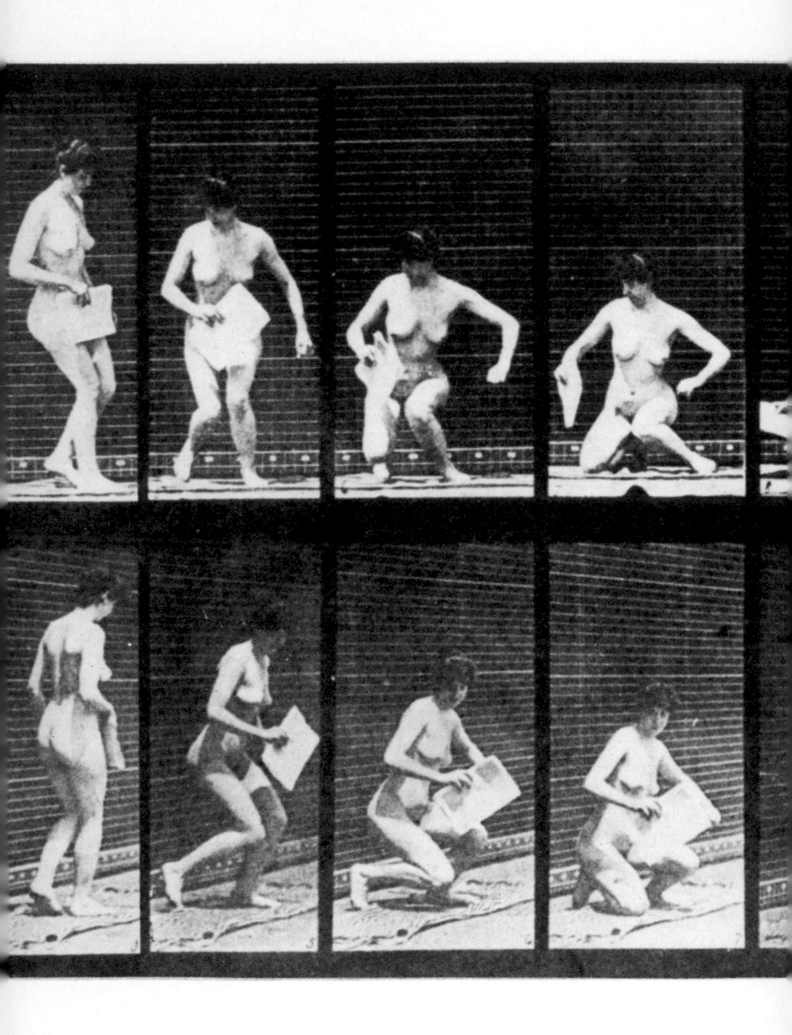

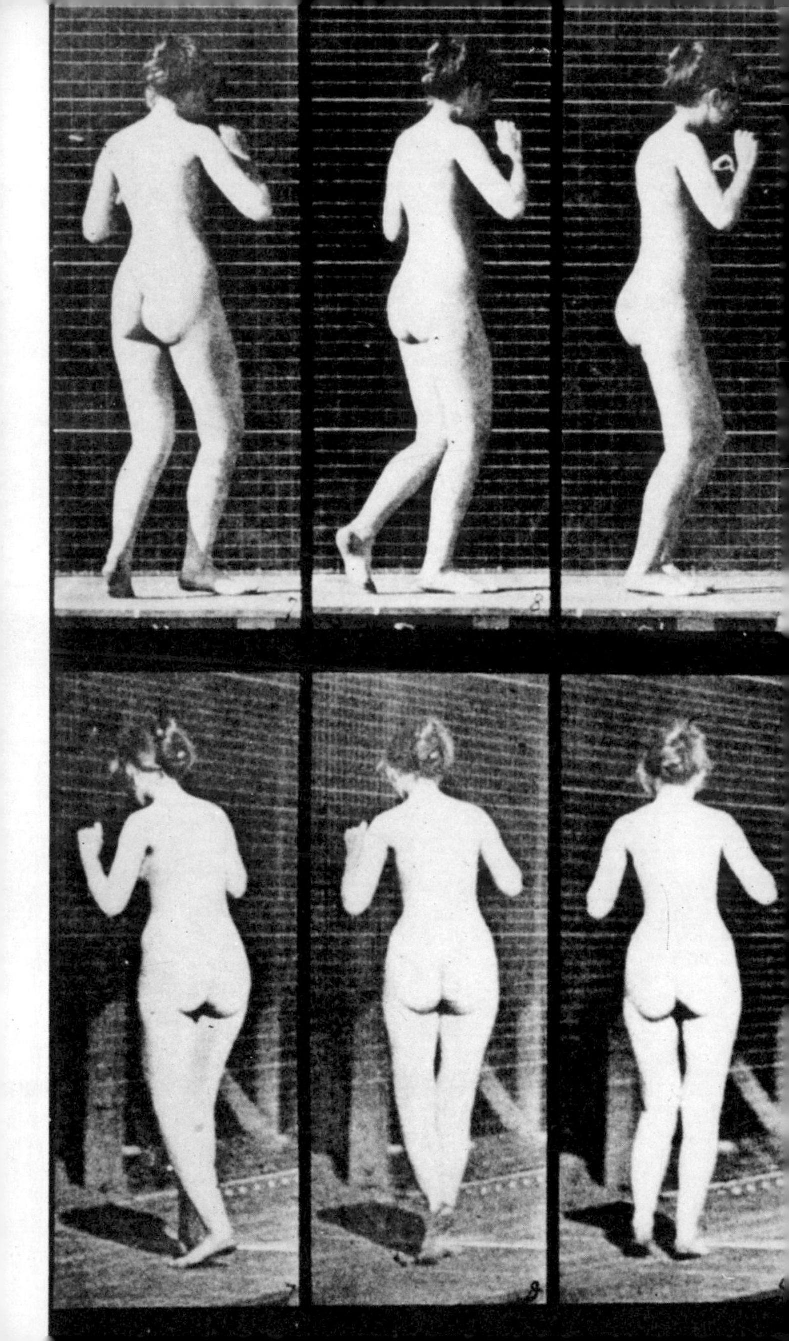

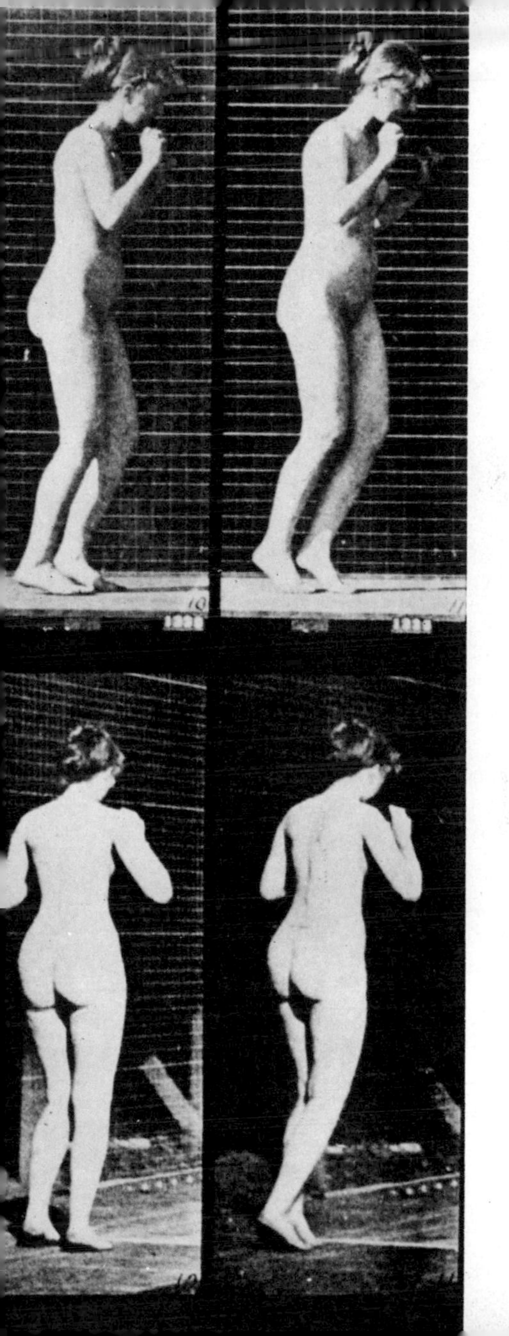

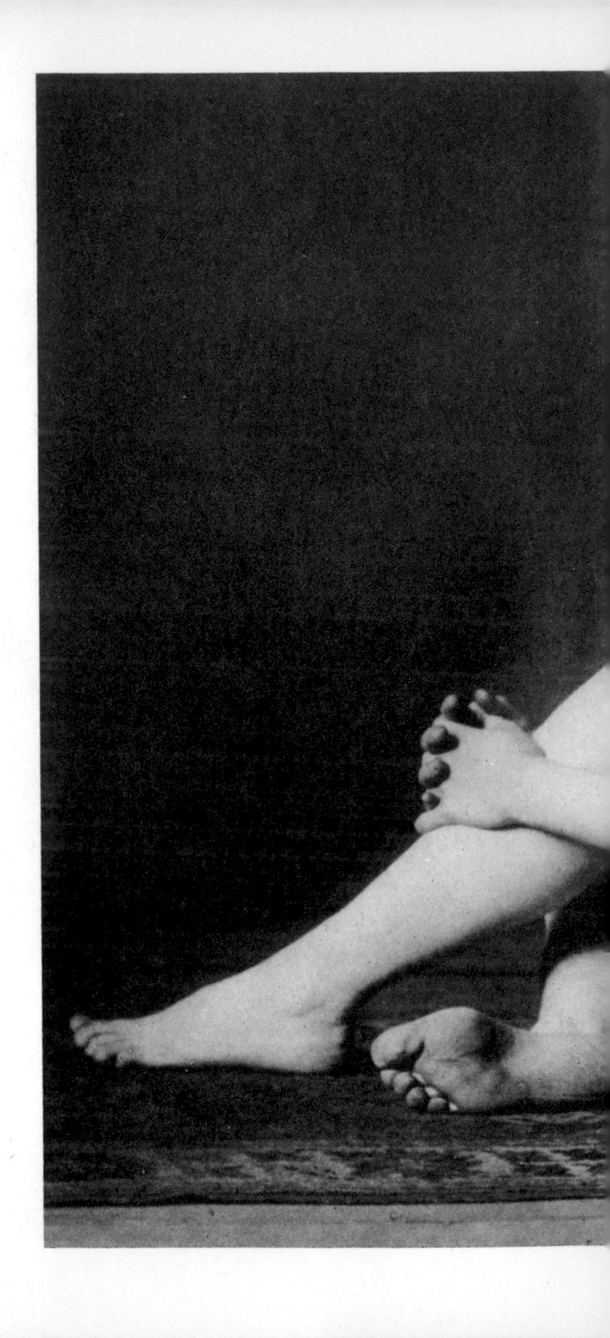

CHARLES SCHENK

In 1902, a large volume of photographs of the nude was published in New York by Charles Schenk, a German-American photographer. Entitled Draperies in Action, the book displayed the ample anatomy of turn-of-the-century models carefully swathed in voluminous, if wrinkled, hangings. The artful poses and flowing drapery seem to suggest a classical point of view, but the fully-fleshed bodies and generous tresses of the ladies are Edwardian beyond all doubt. Since Schenk chose not to accompany his carefully reproduced pictures with a text, we are ignorant of his views on photography and the nude. But the photographs are entrancing and, like the draperies, they can stand alone. In these voluptuous models we have an essential bit of the gay and naughty '90's.

Little is known of Schenk save that he worked in New York at the turn of the century as both photographer and publisher of his own pictures. Besides Draperies in Action, he photographed and published another volume of nudes (Malerische Akstudien) and a large souvenir volume of pictures of the elaborate triumphal arch erected in Brooklyn to honor Admiral Dewey on his victorious return from the Philippines. The arch and the nudes are not dissimilar in their execution and effect. Both are floridly active, even in repose. In this sense, Schenk's photographs are much more typical of the period than those of the contemporary photographers who were to band together as the Photo-Secessionists. When compared to less inspired pictures of the same era (page 10), the naïve vitality of Schenk's nudes becomes more apparent. His adroit use of artificially suspended drapery and dance-like, graceful poses conveys a feeling of movement that is absent in most photographs of the time, especially those of the nude. The nude photographs of the last third of the nineteenth century often aped the lifelessly perfect pseudo-classical academic sculpture of the period.

Schenk's purpose in these nudes resembled the Photo-Secessionists' in that he sought to convey a quality of art. But where the Photo-Secessionists found art in texture and focus, Schenk was content with the traditional classical drapery. Yet the poses are often very good and one can't help wondering what the models would look like without drapery. Nuder is the obvious answer, but they would also lose much of their period charm: the drapery is essential to the models' air of coy innocence. Though Schenk could fail badly, his work is generally of interest. He deserves more fame.

THE PHOTO-SECESSIONISTS:

ROBERT DEMACHY

A. THE STRUGGLE   E. STUDY

FRANK EUGENE

B. LA CIGALE

RENÉE LE BEGUE

C. STUDY

ANNIE BRIGMAN

D. THE CLEFT IN THE ROCK

ALFRED STIEGLITZ and CLARENCE WHITEHEAD

F. TORSO

Founded by Alfred Stieglitz in 1902, the beautifully printed magazine Camera Work published the work of the Photo-Secessionists. Photographs of the nude appeared regularly in Camera Work, usually in portfolios by such photographers as Annie Brigman, Clarence Whitehead, Robert Demachy, Renée Le Begue and Frank Eugene. Though the styles are diverse, the pictures are bound together by their poetic approach to the subject: they are "literary" in that they seek to suggest feelings and associations beyond the actual subject. In quality they range from the banality of Demachy's "Struggle" through the "Studies" of Le Begue to the successful romanticism of Annie Brigman's "Cleft in the Rock." Frank Eugene's "La Cigale" is notable as a prototype of the kind of "salon" nude that was so evident in amateur exhibitions for the next thirty years. The Stieglitz and Whitehead "Torso" contains elements of both the pictorial and straightforward approaches to the nude. It is a successful picture, largely because of the taste and restraint of the photographers: romantic mood is balanced by strong form.

The Photo-Secessionists were articulate but diverse in their theories. Camera Work published numerous articles in which the writers sought to define the elements of the ideal photograph.

"The vagueness of represented forms," wrote Sidney Allen, "runs parallel to certain sound impressions—and that is the reason why modern painters so often make vagueness the vehicle of their emotions. They are aware that mystery dredges deeper than any other emotional suggestion; that it represents to our mind an everlasting enigma which no human thought can solve." The scientific aspect was explored by Roland Rood in "The Philosophy of Focus": ". . . it is through the virtues and weaknesses of the eye that we know and recognize nature, and if the photographer wishes to make us believe that his photographs look like nature, he must subordinate the virtues of his superbly constructed machine and force it to imitate the defects and manners of human vision."

The question of whether or not photography was an art was also discussed. Some thought that it was a close and legitimate relative of painting and drawing. Others that it was an independent art form, no more closely related to painting than to architecture. A few thought the question foolish but believed that photography could be a vehicle of "artistic expression." The burden of art bore heavily on the nude until Alfred Stieglitz and Edward Weston freed her.

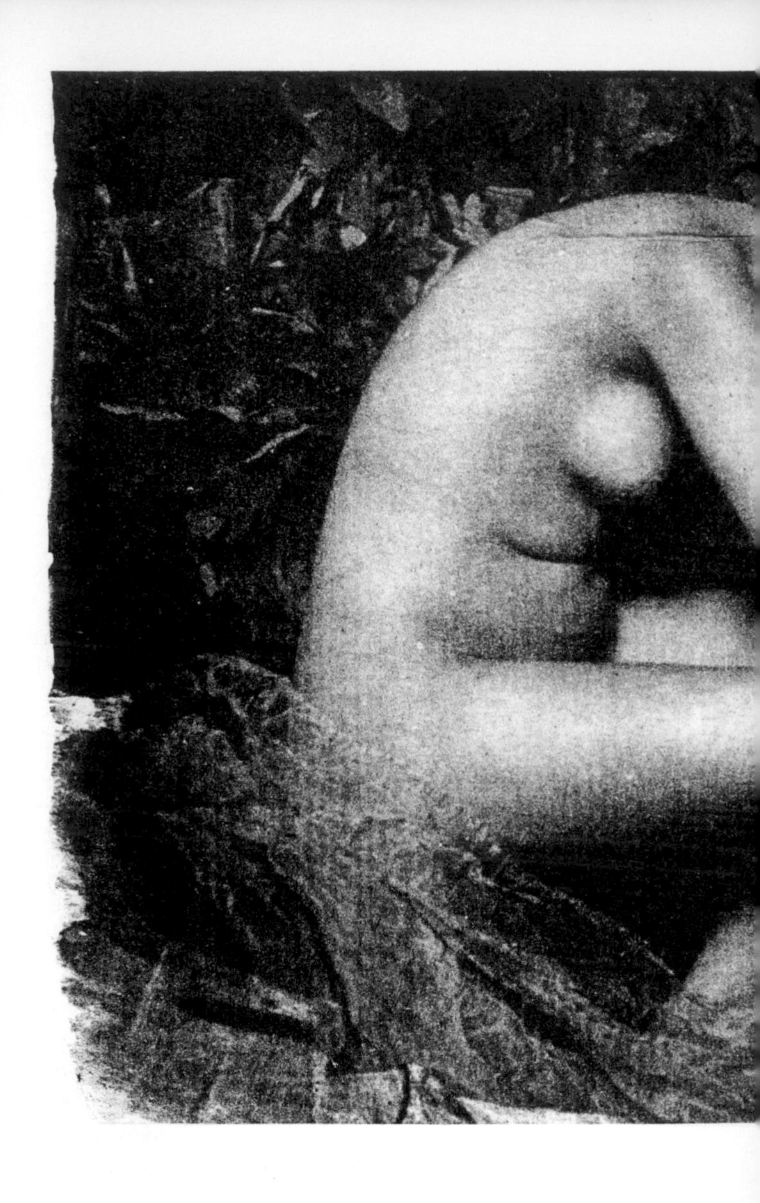

ARNOLD GENTHE

The dancing nudes of Arnold Genthe were photographed in the second decade of this century, when the popularity of both "the dance" and Genthe were at their height. Isadora Duncan had overwhelmed culture-conscious America with her free-flowing dance movements, and Genthe had overwhelmed her with his photographs: "This is not a photograph," she cried on seeing his first portrait of her, "it is a miracle!" Though the softly focused images of Genthe's pictures no longer seem exactly miracles, they do still retain a charming blitheness of form. And Genthe's dancers give an impression of movement not usually found in photographs of the dance taken before or since.

Arnold Genthe, a tall, handsome, and courtly gentleman, had by 1916 become a famous and fashionable photographer. In that year his Book of the Dance appeared, and among its many photographs of famous dancers was a portfolio of "classical" dancing nudes. The models were anonymous, but the poses were obviously inspired by the dance movements of Isadora Duncan and her disciples. Genthe had become the foremost photographer of the dance—his first successful portrait of the notoriously inaccessible (to photographers) Isadora had been followed by many pictures of her and other dancers. Since Isadora stressed the natural beauty of the body, it was inevitable that Genthe would photographically combine the nude and the dance. Like Schenk, he uses drapery, but more judiciously. Like the Photo-Secessionists, his pictures are softly focused—photography had not yet been entirely freed from the onus of art.

Genthe was born in Germany and educated to be a scholar; he received a Ph.D. in classical philology before emigrating to San Francisco. There he became a tutor to the child of a wealthy German. Genthe was fascinated by the city, especially its Chinatown, and purchased a camera to record it. His pictures of youthful San Francisco are still famous and include striking photos of the devastation caused by the great earthquake of 1906. His tutorial duties completed, Genthe set himself up as a portrait photographer. His skill and fashionable connections soon brought success. He eventually moved to New York, where he became a leading magazine and advertising photographer while continuing to take his famous (and expensive) portraits. His studio in midtown Manhattan was visited by the rich and famous: a Genthe portrait had by now become an essential status symbol. But through it all the dance remained his greatest interest.

EDWARD WESTON

Edward Weston brought to the nude all of the clarity of vision and simplicity of technique that characterized his life and work. Nature and the elemental forms of life were his inspiration and he saw them with a power unmatched by any other photographer. Though his earliest nudes reflect the popular soft focus of the Photo-Secessionists, he rapidly discovered the infinite variety of clearly perceived natural forms. By the late 1920's he had become interested in the resemblances, or "affinities," of these natural forms to the point of abstraction. The nudes of this period are not wholly seen by the viewer. A partial view is presented to us, so strongly suggestive of related forms that we are unsure of the exact subject: we may see a cleft peach or a woman's buttocks, according to our predilections. The visually sophisticated will see both, which was exactly Weston's intention. Though he never lost this interest in the affinities and symbolic values of forms, he turned in his later years to a fuller portrayal of nature, especially the nude. The period 1932-1936 was a time when Weston fully integrated his love for abstract form with a larger vision. The finest examples of his work during this period are the nudes done in the open air and sunlight of his Pacific Coast home.

What concerned Weston most was his vision, and to this end he simplified and refined photographic technique to its most basic elements. A large view camera, a tripod, and an exposure meter were the tools he used with great refinement and precision. Weston began his photographic career as a portrait photographer, and the earlier nudes were often done in his studio by northlight (or occasionally artificial light). Natural sunlight, direct or diffused, eventually became his favored source and inspiration; in later photographs not even a reflector was used. All negatives were developed in a tray or tank by inspection and all prints were made by direct contact. Within this elementary framework Weston, a master craftsman, produced superbly balanced prints and negatives.

The nudes of Edward Weston are probably better known to the general public than those of any other photographer. They were certainly instrumental in bringing about the current acceptance of the nude as a legitimate subject of photography. Yet Weston's income never matched his eminence and in this fact lies one of the paradoxes of professional photography: financial success in photography is not likely to follow the pursuit of a personal vision such as Weston's.

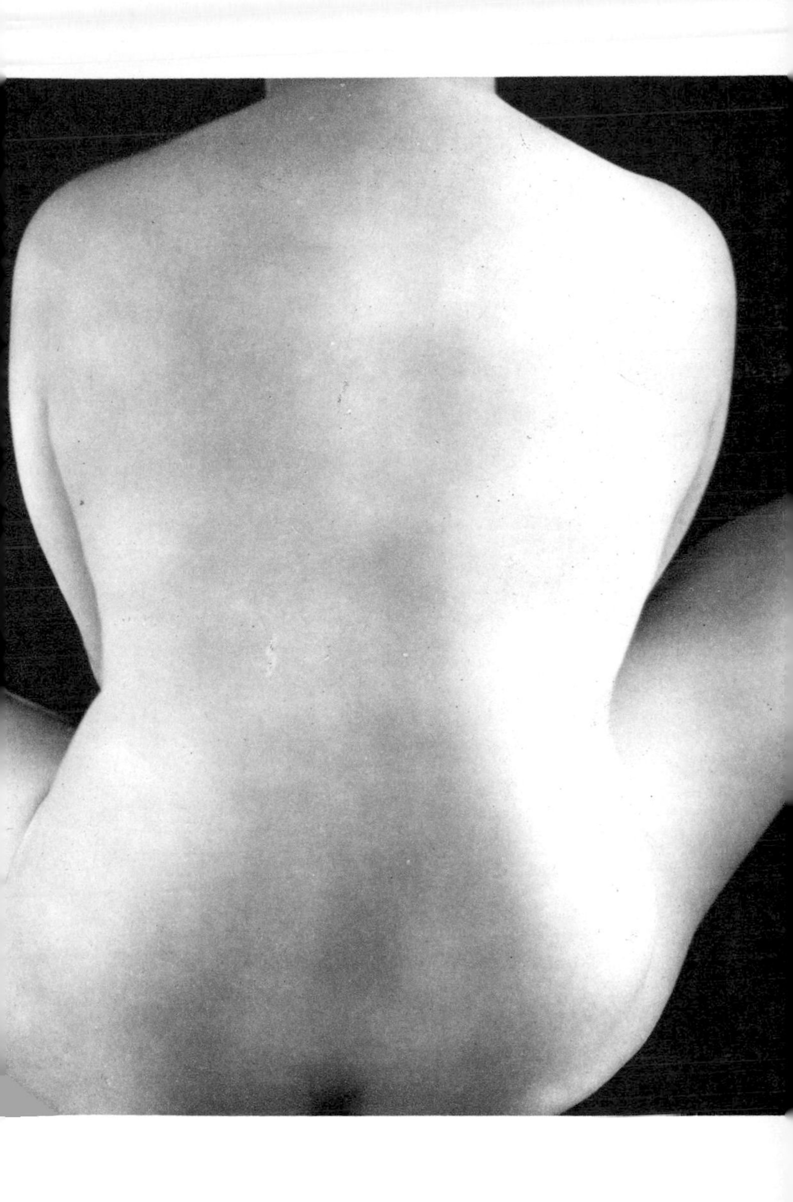

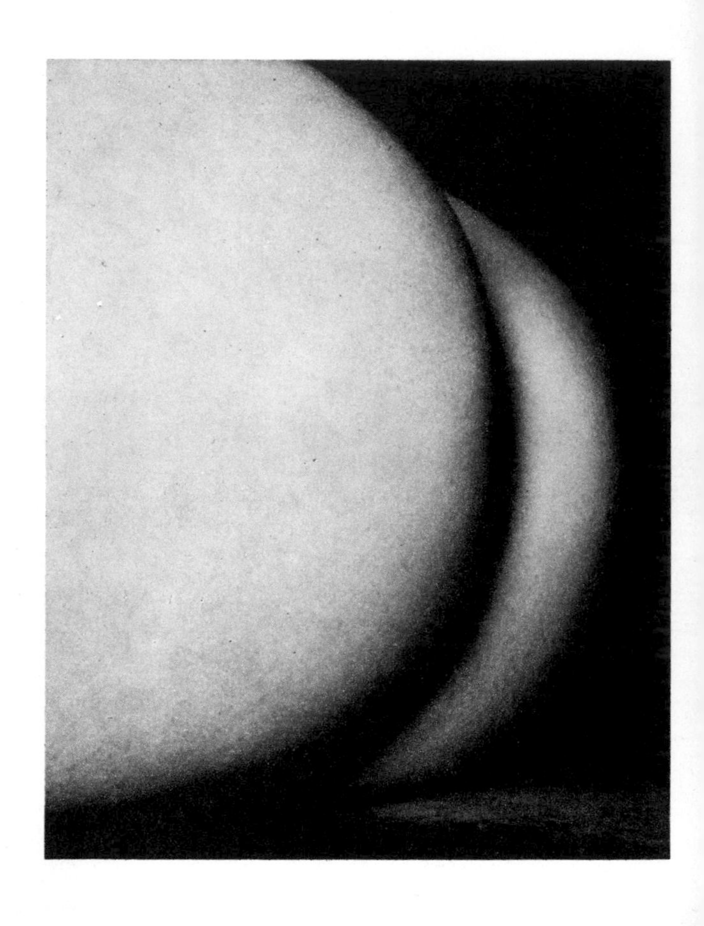

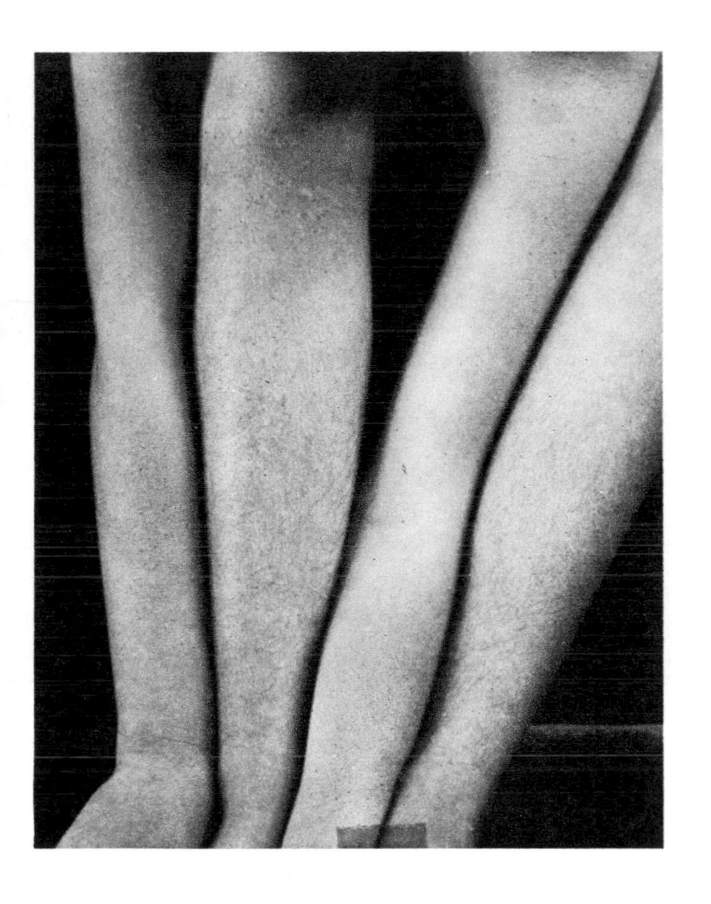

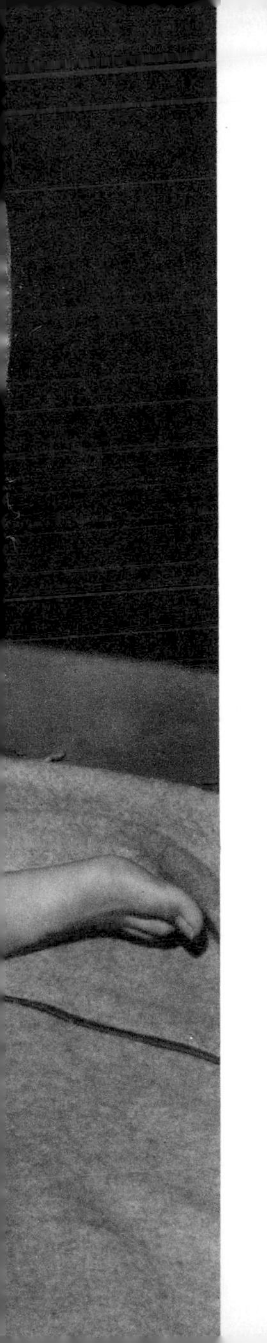

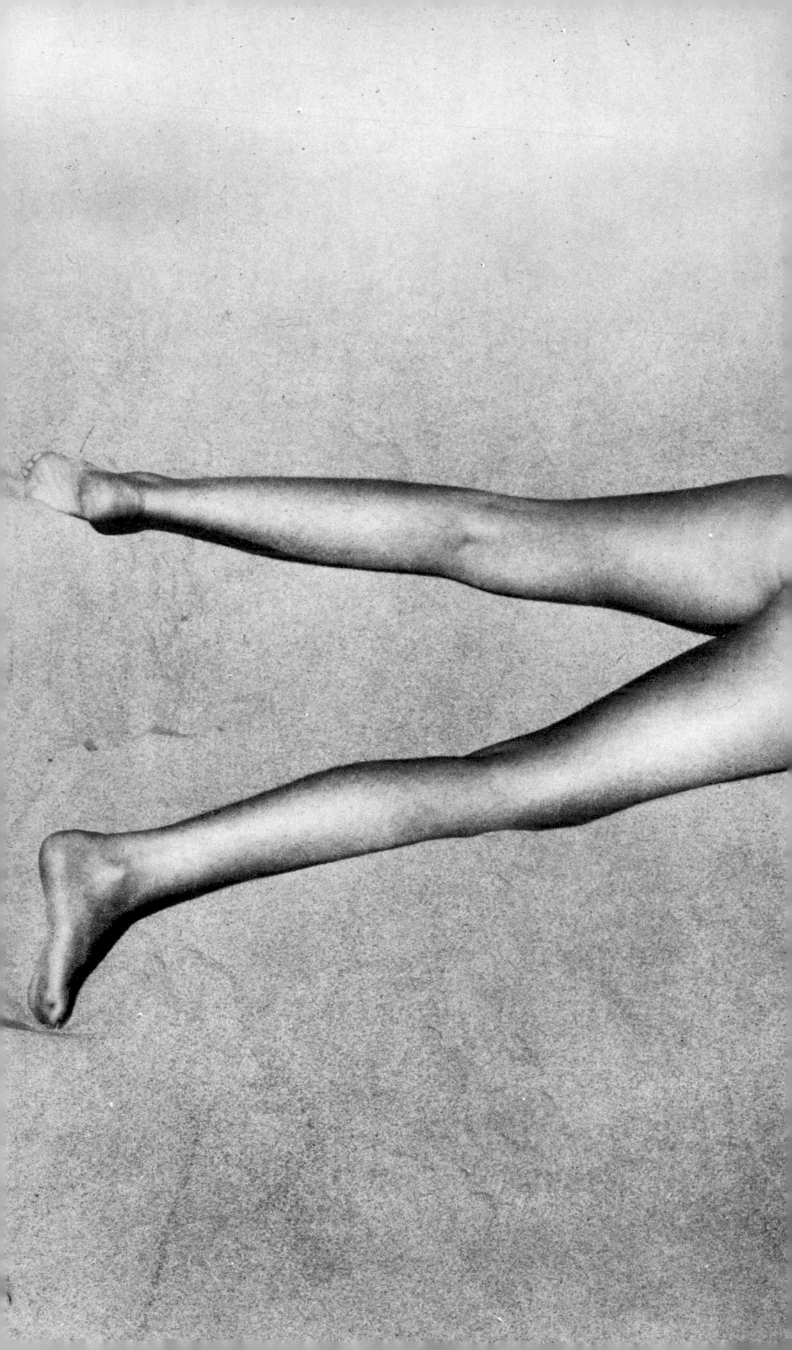

HARRY CALLAHAN

Line and design, light and dark, the mysterious in the commonplace—these are the concerns and style of Harry Callahan. In his photographs the nude becomes an enigmatic element of composition. She never speaks solely of herself, yet she is never obscured. Callahan is a photographer who has made the nude a touchstone to the designs of nature and man. He has found in her a mysterious modesty and elusiveness. His nudes are always psychologically remote, regardless of their physical proximity; and like Edward Weston, he has found in their contours the suggestion of other forms and lines.

The opening photograph of this portfolio at first glance seems straightforward: a nude reclining on the grass of a glade. Yet the composition is formal and centered to a degree that surpasses simple reality. Also, why (as in most of Callahan's photographs) has the nude turned her back to us? She is there but remote—not to be disturbed, like some mythical being. We have come upon her unaware, and should she sense us, she will vanish.

Again we see her, indisputably the same woman, as she contemplates a sea so flat and still it could be a desert. In her mysterious motionlessness she unites the land and sky, her torso bridging the sea. Her figure and its shadow form an angle of humanity in a seemingly lifeless vista of sea and sand.

In the next two photographs the nude affirms her individuality and femininity with her face. Yet, as she rises from the water, a reluctant Venus, she averts her eyes: the dreaming gaze of Botticelli's goddess is seen here again. In intimacy she also achieves a kind of anonymity: even with the sleeping child her head is characteristically hidden.

Finally, in the last three photographs, the nude has merged with light and line to become design. But, paradoxically, she continues to assert her undoubted femininity. Callahan never completely subordinates the nude to design.

Harry Callahan has devoted much of his career to teaching photography at advanced schools of design in the United States. In these positions he has been able to pursue his personal interests to an unusual degree. He has written: "The only reason that I consciously know for taking these pictures is because photography enriches my life. This has been true for the past and I hope for the future. After the pictures are made and affect other people, I am encouraged in my continuing." Now on the faculty of The Rhode Island School of Design, Callahan continues his photographic explorations of the many forms of nature and the nude.

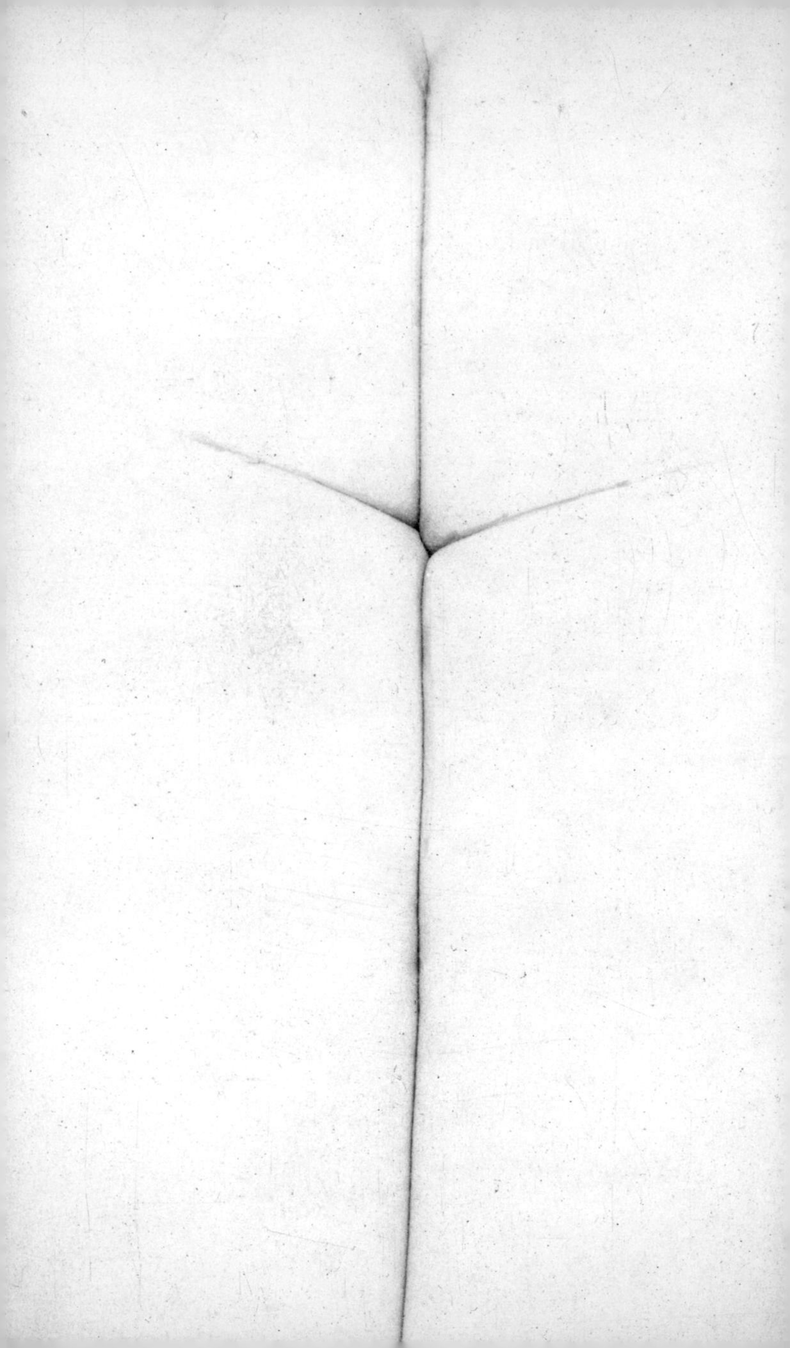

EMMANUEL SOUGEZ

For the first several decades of this century the naughty young beauties drawn for the French magazine La Vie Parisienne were familiar figures as they gamboled in dishabille or less in the pages of that venerable document of joie de vivre. The nudes of the Parisian photographer Emmanuel Sougez are the photographic cousins of those pen and ink coquettes. But Sougez's nudes are more real and, of necessity, more modest. They seem to shrink before our admiring gaze (shrink, not flee) and they silently beseech us to be gentle. They are purely and simply feminine. Though meant to be sexually admired, they represent an older, more discreet, view of woman; Sougez's nudes are closer in character to the models of Durieu than to the aggressively forthright nude "playmates" of today's magazine fold-outs. In their finest moments (as in the reclining nudes of the last two spreads) they suggest the atmosphere of paintings by the eighteenth-century artists Fragonard and Boucher. Above all, Sougez's nudes represent an ideal of femininity. Form in these photographs is always soft and feminine always a component of what is first of all an individual and beautiful woman. It is their idealization that distinguishes these nudes from the myriad of simply illustrative nudes produced by other rather less *imaginative photographers during the same period.*

Sougez, who was born in Bordeaux in 1889, attended the École des Beaux-Arts as a youth, and this experience is apparent in his photographs. In art school he avoided the contemporary academic approach to the nude and applied to the study of the human body the same technique he used for all other subjects. This technique was characterized by careful composition, harmonious line, and clarity of form. These characteristics are present in his photographs and his intention still remains the same: he believes that a beautiful body should not be photographed differently than a Doric column, for example. Sougez's approach does not, however, submerge the individual femininity of his models: form is never completely dominant. He has expressed his belief that it is more in his choice of subject matter and angles of view than by a particular technique that the photographer gives to his pictures the stamp of his personality.

Throughout his long career, Emmanuel Sougez has distinguished himself not only as a photographer but also as a writer on the subject. Since 1930 he has published articles and illustrated works on the art and technique of photography, especially color and the application of photography to the graphic arts.

FERENC
BERKO

Ferenc Berko has restlessly explored the many aspects of photography. Like others, he has often turned to the nude for her beauty and challenge. His pictures show his changing attitude toward the subject and in some ways reflect the styles of many other (and less talented) photographers of the last three decades. That is to say, Berko has been concerned with the same problems that have confronted the majority of those who have photographed the nude in our time: the difficulty of blending form with individuality, mood with veracity. These are formidable problems if the photographer is unsure of his attitude or intention; no other subject is so indicative of the photographer's taste and talent as the nude. The chronological succession of Berko's nudes shows the evolution of his vision of her. Though his approach varies, Berko's taste and technique remain fine throughout.

The earliest nudes were photographed both outdoors and in the studio. There is a strong emphasis on the female torso itself —rarely is a face seen. In these pictures mood is suggested by lighting and the use of materials of contrasting texture. The general approach is romantic rather than realistic. Berko's famous solarizations of the nude are products of the darkroom and are intentionally the antithesis of "straight" photography. Man Ray and others had used the technique with varying degrees of moderation, but Berko's come just short of abstraction. Darkroom manipulation of negative and print was nothing new, of course: the Photo-Secessionists (and many nineteenth-century photographers before them) had experimented freely. What distinguishes the solarizations from such earlier work is their photographic, rather than "artistic," intent and result. Though they are far removed from the "pure" photographic approach to the nude of Edward Weston, they are, nevertheless, valid and effective pictures. They are expressions of form through photographic means; mood and individuality are reduced to a minimum here.

Berko's most recent photographs of the nude, the culmination of his earlier experiments, are less abstract than the solarizations, but are still inclined to distillation of line and form It is the simplification of black and white. Yet the nude is still recognizably and individually present. She has not become a symbol or related form, yet her image has been refined to its basic elements. Ferenc Berko, whose varied photographic career includes industrial and cinema work, continues to find the nude an inspiring subject in all of her varied manifestations.

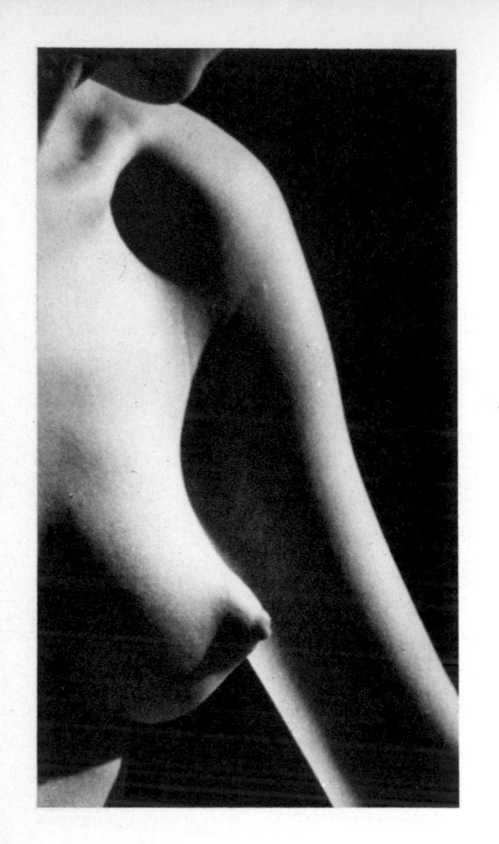

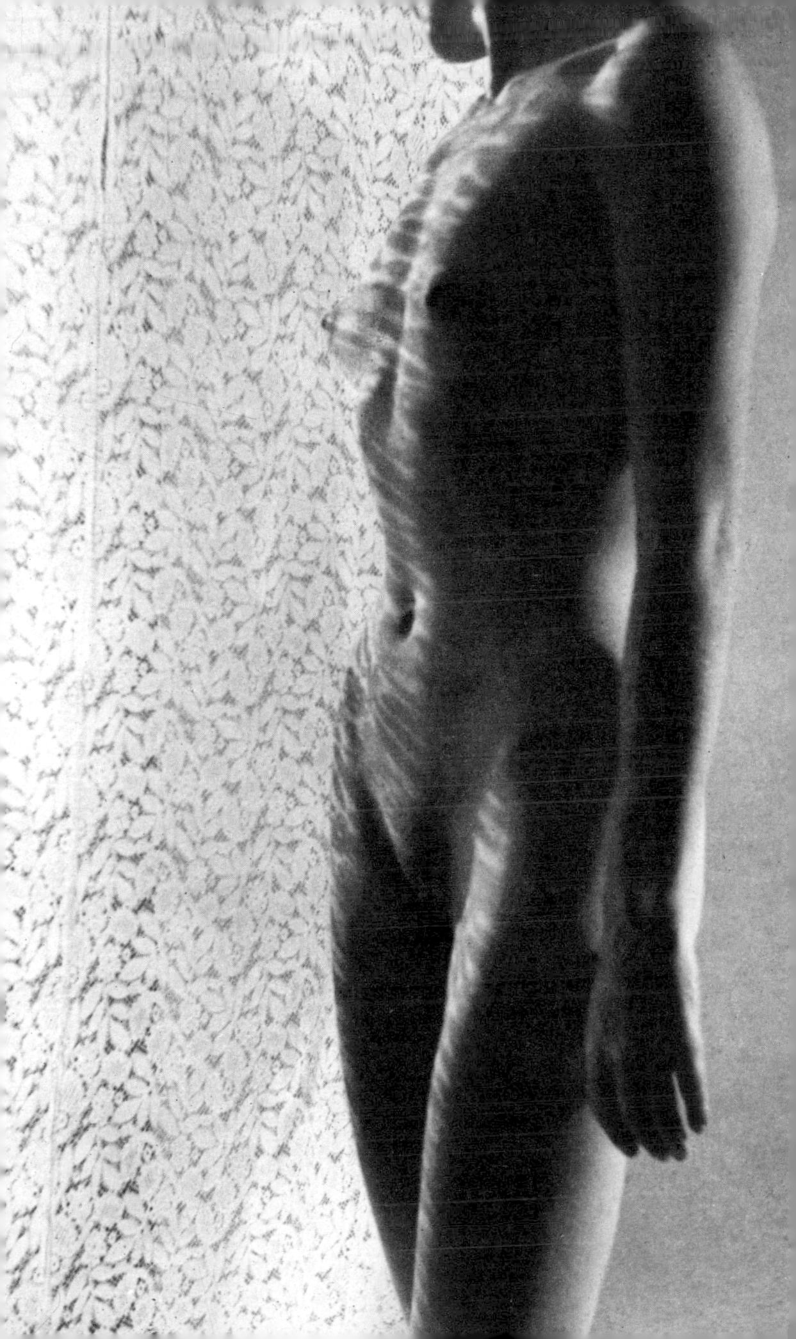

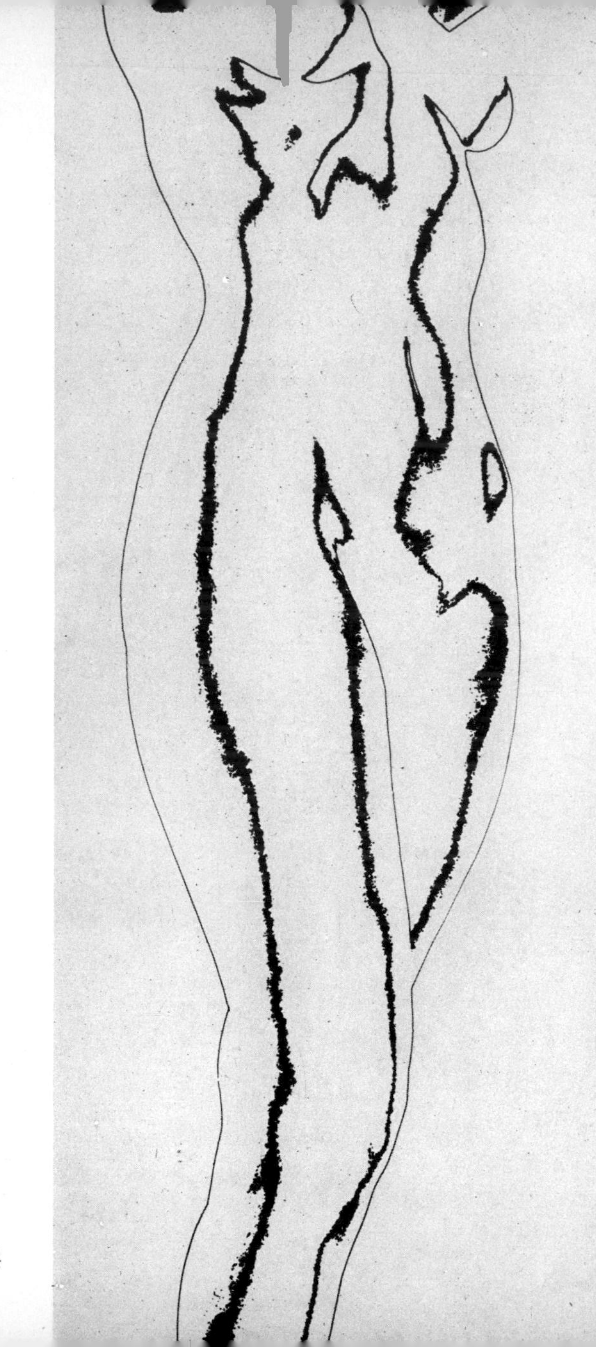

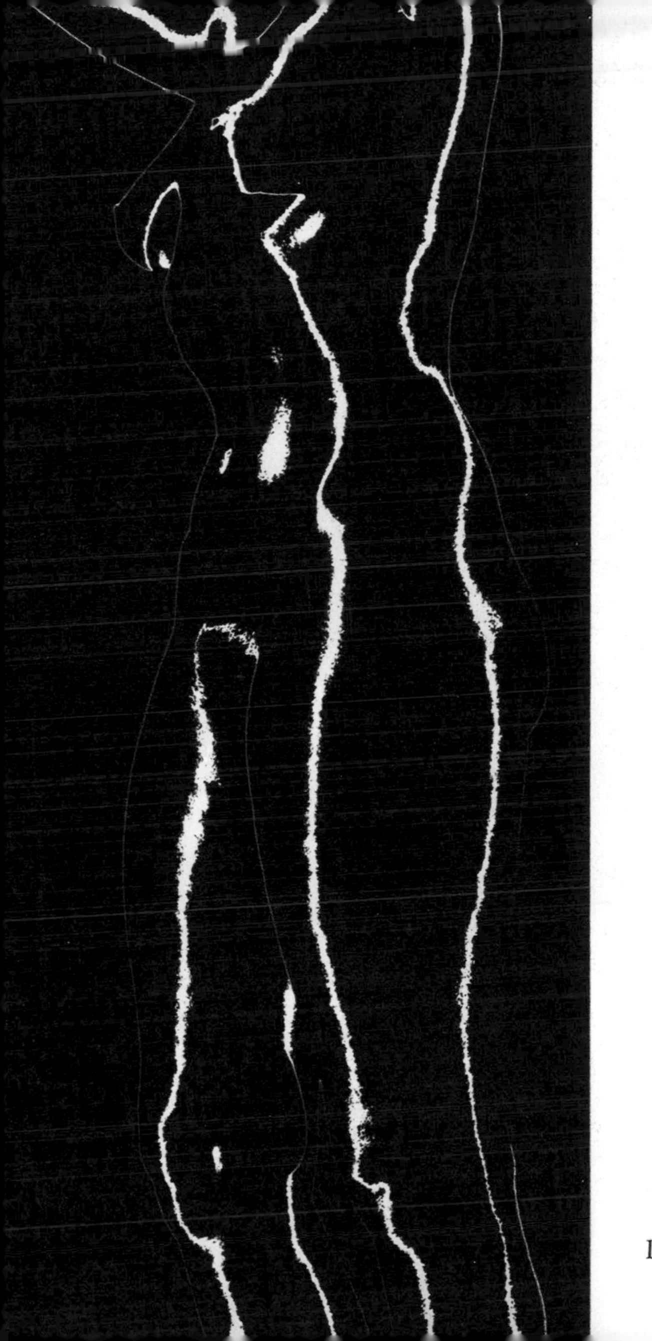

LUCIEN CLERGUE

The vital nudes that erupt from the sea in Lucien Clergue's famous photographs of "Nus de la Mer" have been praised by Picasso ("Pictures worthy of Renoir's signature.") and Jean Cocteau ("Clergue has witnessed the birth of Aphrodite."). They have inspired and illustrated a book of poems by the eminent French poet Paul Eluard, Corps Memorables. They are certainly very good pictures and the measure of Clergue's achievement is that he has approached a photographic cliché (nude and sea) and produced powerful and individual photographs.

Cocteau's simile seems closer to the mark than Picasso's. We do seem to witness the birth of Aphrodite in each picture. The myth of the love goddess's birth from the sea has inspired countless artists for thousands of years. Photographers have plunged the nude into water with varying degrees of success. What distinguishes Clergue's pictures is their primal vitality. They are of one woman and all women: Aphrodite. The forms are voluptuous and anonymous, essentially female. The foaming sea from which they emerge seems to animate them. They are midway between nature and humanity.

Clergue lives in the city where he was born in 1934, ancient

Arles in southern France. The radiant climate and proximity of the Mediterranean have naturally led him to photograph the forms of life (and death) found at the edge of the sea. Clergue has a poet's interest in death: dead birds and animals embedded in the marshes of the Camargue, even the dead water and plants of the marsh itself, have been strikingly photographed by him. It was necessary to balance such death with vitality and movement. The nudes were Clergue's answer. They are an affirmation of life, and their symbolic and poetic content strengthens rather than dilutes their appeal. This does not always happen. In a lesser photographer's work the weight of symbol and allegory usually crushes an already frail vision. Clergue's photographs have an instantaneous appeal—we are struck by the beautifully sensuous form of the nude itself before we begin to draw literary inferences. These inferences strengthen rather than support or weaken the picture. Again the lesson of Weston is clear: form is essential. The forms of Clergue's nudes are made more universal by the elimination of their faces. Yet the torsos speak intimately for themselves. This is a quality of the photographed nude alone.

Clergue's nudes of the sea prove that the nude can be blended with nature effectively and enhancingly. It is her element.

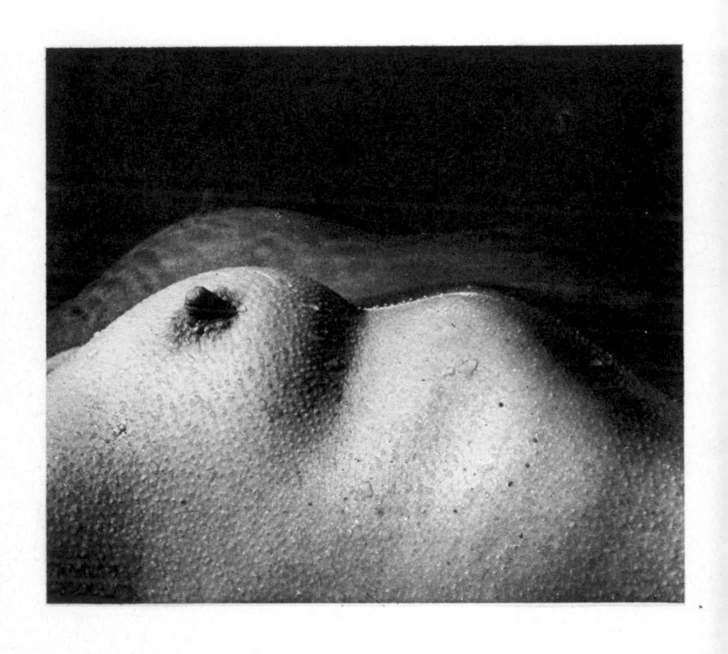

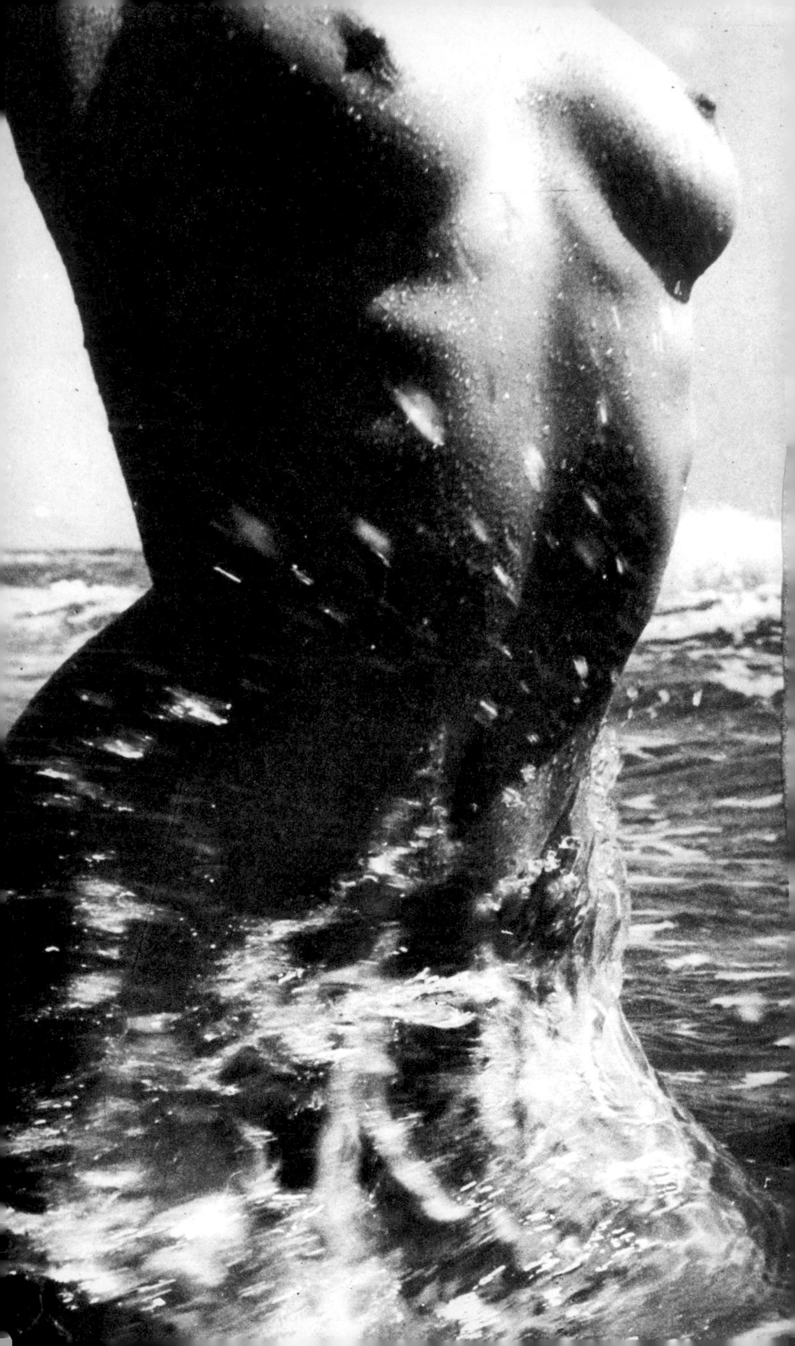

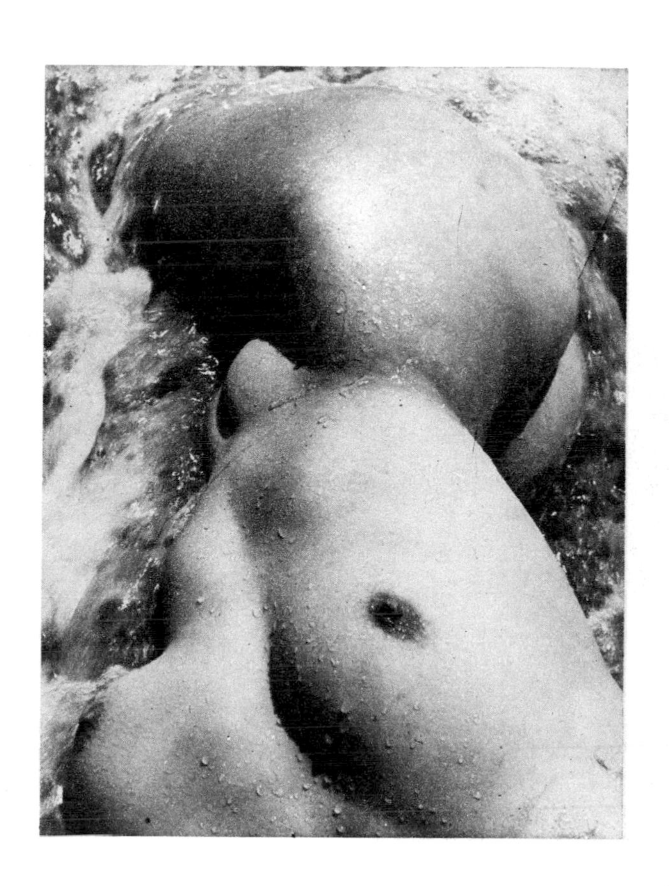

RUTH BERNHARD

There have been several distinguished woman photographers of the nude in this emancipated century, notably Emy Andriesse of Holland, and Nell Dorr and Ruth Bernhard of the United States. Miss Bernhard's work is probably the most widely known, her photographs having appeared regularly in magazines and books over the last three decades. Her style is distinctive and her photographs maintain a fine balance between strong form and gentle femininity. She has written of her interest in the nude: "Every artist, in a sense, is a missionary. He tries to convey a message to his fellow man—he communicates the awesome presence of truth and beauty he discovers in the world around him, in its lakes and mountains, trees, rocks and plants, in its living creatures.

"Down through the centuries poets, sculptors, painters, and now photographers, have also been striving to grasp and immortalize the beauty of the human body, both male and female.

"I see in these forms the elemental relationship to the large forms of nature; a sense of strength like a rock—fluidity like water—space like a mountain range.

"If I have chosen the female form in particular, it is because beauty has been debased and exploited in our sensual twentieth

century. We seem to have a need to turn innocent nature into evil ugliness by the twist of the mind. Woman has been the target of much that is sordid and cheap, especially in photography. To raise, to elevate, to endorse with timeless reverence the image of woman, has been my mission—the reason for my work which you see here."

Ruth Bernhard likes to contrast the curving lines and rounded forms of her models with impersonal, unnatural straight lines and rectangular forms. By these means the gently swelling, feminine contours of her subjects are emphasized without undue stress or contortion. The pleasingly pear-shaped derrière perched on the edge of a swimming pool in the opening photograph is emphatically feminine. The long, golden hair of the model has a texture and presence of its own, while it enhances the torso. The delicacy of this picture contrasts with the massive monumentality of the kneeling figure shown on page 132 (bottom). Here femininity is subservient to powerful form. The rather contrived pose of the model on page 134 is alleviated by her almost perfect figure and the complimentary lighting. It is, however, in the photographs on pages 133 and 136 that Ruth Bernhard most characteristically blends impersonal formality with personal form.

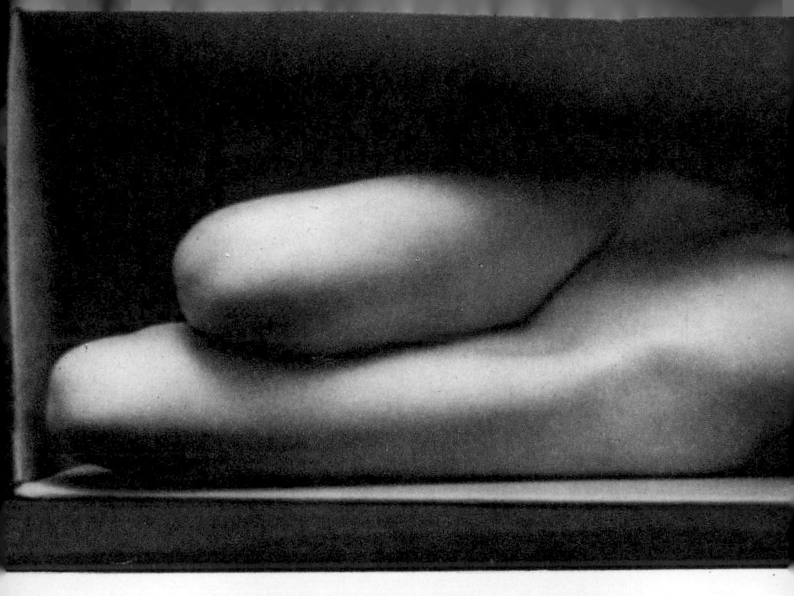

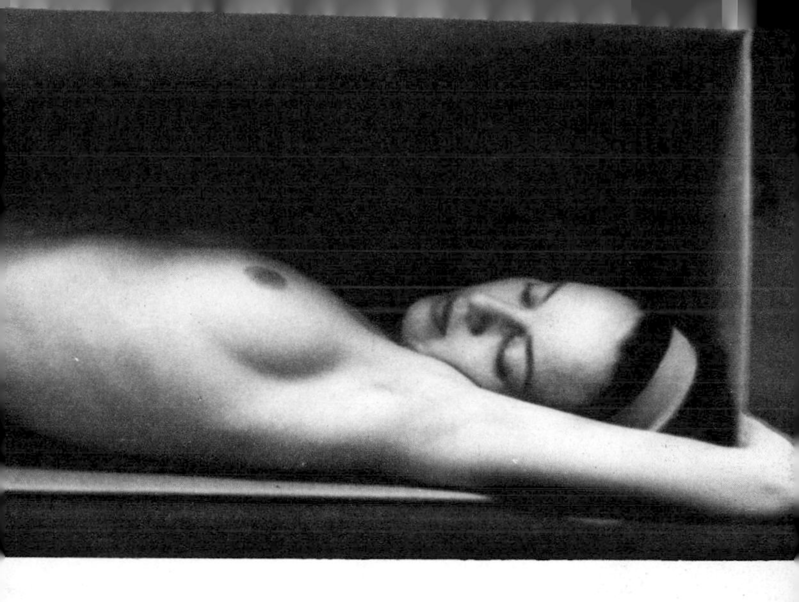

RENÉ GROEBLI

A number of years ago a young Swiss photographer and his new bride made a honeymoon journey through France. In that romantic country they found that Eros attended even the humblest of hotel rooms. The photographer, René Groebli, chose to record this beginning event in their lives and in doing so, produced a series of sensitive photographs that are a tour de force in good taste. In his book Vision of Love, from which these pictures were selected, Groebli has managed to convey with intimacy the beauty of a woman in love. He has somehow avoided all of the traps into which any would-be observer of love may fall. The nude here is not only a feminine form but is also a particular woman, closely observed. Yet, as in all fine photographs of the nude, her identity is never the dominant factor of her presence. In the darkened hotel room her figure is caught sensitively as she prepares for bed. The effect is not of a striptease—each photographed movement has its own value and beauty. The story is cumulative rather than consecutive in its mood and telling. It is romantic in the sense that the situation is inherently romantic. This romanticism is matched (but not overemphasized) by the subdued light and generally soft focus of the photographs. Altogether, Groebli's sequence of pictures is a memorable and unusual discovery of the nude in a realistic setting.

When the earliest photographers began to portray the nude, she was, as we have seen, invariably imagined and displayed within the static confines of "fine art." Any hint of realism was to be shunned, both aesthetically and morally. Through the period of the Photo-Secessionists in the early part of this century this attitude persisted. In addition, the idea of such a subject as Groebli's was technically unfeasible. Only with the development of the miniature camera and fast film, along with a broadening of our moral outlook, have such photographs become possible and acceptable. The work of photographers like René Groebli has been crucial in bringing about the public acceptance of such picture stories and in increasing the awareness of the aesthetic possibilities of the camera.

Today René Groebli is one of the leading advertising and industrial photographers in Switzerland. He is also famous for his imaginative use of color in his pictures. Though his photo-reportage is now of necessity usually limited to commercial subjects, he continues to find the feminine nude a source of photographic inspiration, basic yet always challenging.

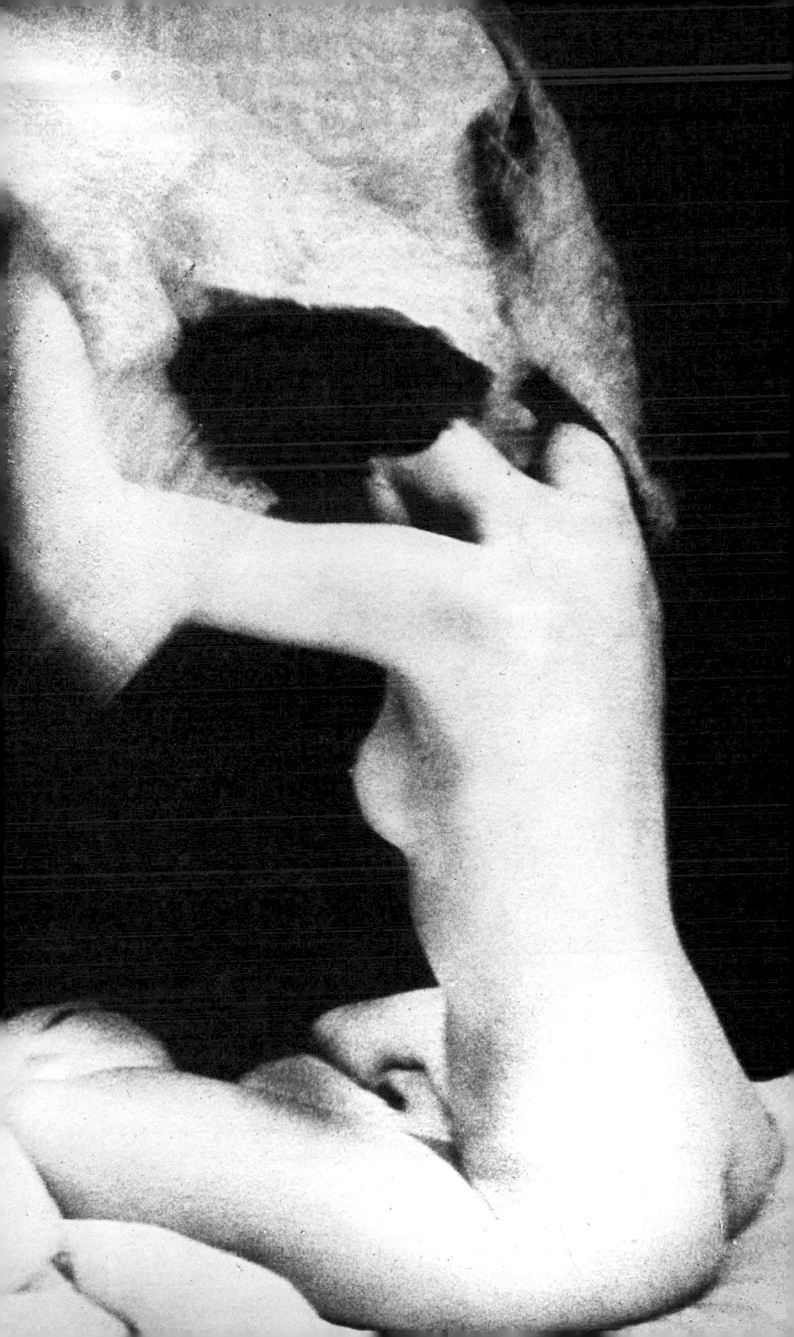

JEANLOUP SIEFF

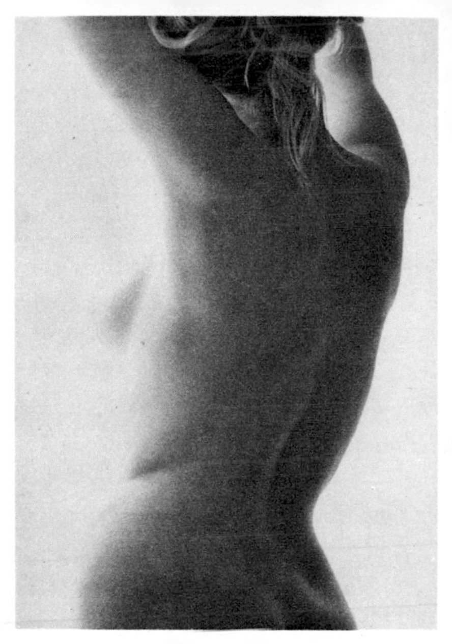

It is a perplexing fact that very few fashion photographers have pictured the nude extensively or significantly. It seems reasonable to expect that photographers who spend most of their working hours photographing fashionably beautiful women would naturally become interested in the fundamentals of their subjects. But such is not the case. The famous exceptions of Erwin Blumenfeld, John Rawlings, and Irving Penn only prove the rule. It is probable that most fashion photographers have occasionally taken pictures of the nude, but comparatively few notable ones have come to light. The reasons for this lack are not readily apparent, but certainly not all fashion photographers have had the two necessary qualities of the best portrayers of the nude: a sense of basic form and an interest in woman as an individual. Among the best younger fashion photographers today, the Frenchman Jeanloup Sieff combines these qualities with a warmth and vivacity that is apparent in all of his pictures, whether fashion or journalistic. He has brought to fashion the sensitive eye of a photojournalist; his photographs of models are not sterile poses but are lively portrayals of interesting girls wearing fine clothes.

Most of the photographs in this portfolio were taken as studies for an advertising assignment. Sieff has been interested in the subject of the nude throughout his career thus far and has produced a number of pictures notable for their effective blending of form and composition with a perceptive feeling of intimacy. The assignment to photograph a nude suitable for general publication in an advertisement and yet revealingly intimate was a difficult one; Sieff made many such studies preparatory to the final published picture. What these studies have in common is a fine combination of strong form and gracefully individual femininity: the model retains her identity as a particular woman even when her face is not shown. This effect is accomplished by a skillful capturing of poses in a softly directional light that seems to embrace the figure. Sieff's portrayal of the nude is far removed from the bland directness of Durieu's Parisian models of over a century ago. The difference is not entirely due to the advances in photographic technique. As we have seen, the concept of the nude at the inception of photography was inherited from contemporary academic art: the nude must be "elevated" to the realm of the exotic, classical, or sentimental—she must not be herself. The great development of the photographic nude "as she is" is exemplified by Sieff.

CHARLES SWEDLUND

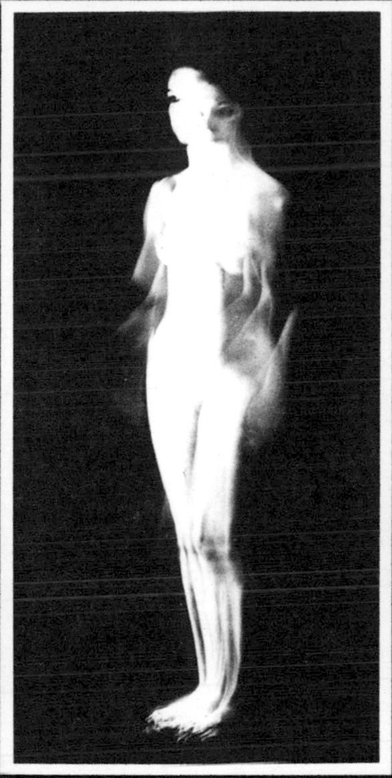

Where Edward Weston sought symbolic form, Charles Swedlund has created it. Swedlund's methods are far removed from Weston's, in that he uses camera and darkroom manipulation to bring about his effects. Only in his meticulous photographic technique does he follow Weston's tradition. Yet his nudes are photographic in intent and result. Swedlund has written of his aims and methods: "I worked in a completely 'unclassical' way, using, as instruments of discovery, many of the facets of the camera and the photographic process—multiple exposure, high-contrast film, slow shutter speeds, and out-of-focus images. At first I shot out-of-doors, in an exploratory spirit, to see what would happen, what could happen. Gradually I grew dissatisfied because there was not enough control, and I turned to the severely controlled conditions of the studio and single subject material—the nude figure. I could now concentrate on the form-to-be-made with a fair expectation of success."

When looking at these nudes of Charles Swedlund, it is impossible to escape their psychological connotations. Each picture is both an aesthetically pleasing form and a complexly suggestive symbol. The opening photograph is a ghostly X-ray of a beautiful girl. She is moving in her motionlessness—shadowy form and bodily substance seem to blend and dissolve uncertainly. And in all of the other photographs of the nude by Swedlund we encounter similar ambiguities of form and meaning. Our individual response to these pictures is subjective in its details, but the basic factor is certainly sexual.

Sex is always present in the nude. The symbolic nudes of Swedlund are distillations of that element. By juxtaposition the photographs can shed light on each other's meaning. The two pictures on the first spread could be reality and dream: the tight substantial shame of the sitting figure is related to the shadowy sexuality of the striding nude beside it. The multiple exposures of the two photographs on the next spread serve to emphasize rather than diminish the voluptuous solidity of the model. The effect is akin to cubistic painting: the prismatic blending of the lines and planes of the multiple figures deepens rather than diminishes space and substance. Finally, on the last spread, the nude subject has been photographically anatomized and reconstructed into a semi-abstract object. The result of such a process can easily be vulgar or boring, but when done with wit and sensitivity, as here, it can be revealingly symbolic, while remaining strikingly photographic and original.

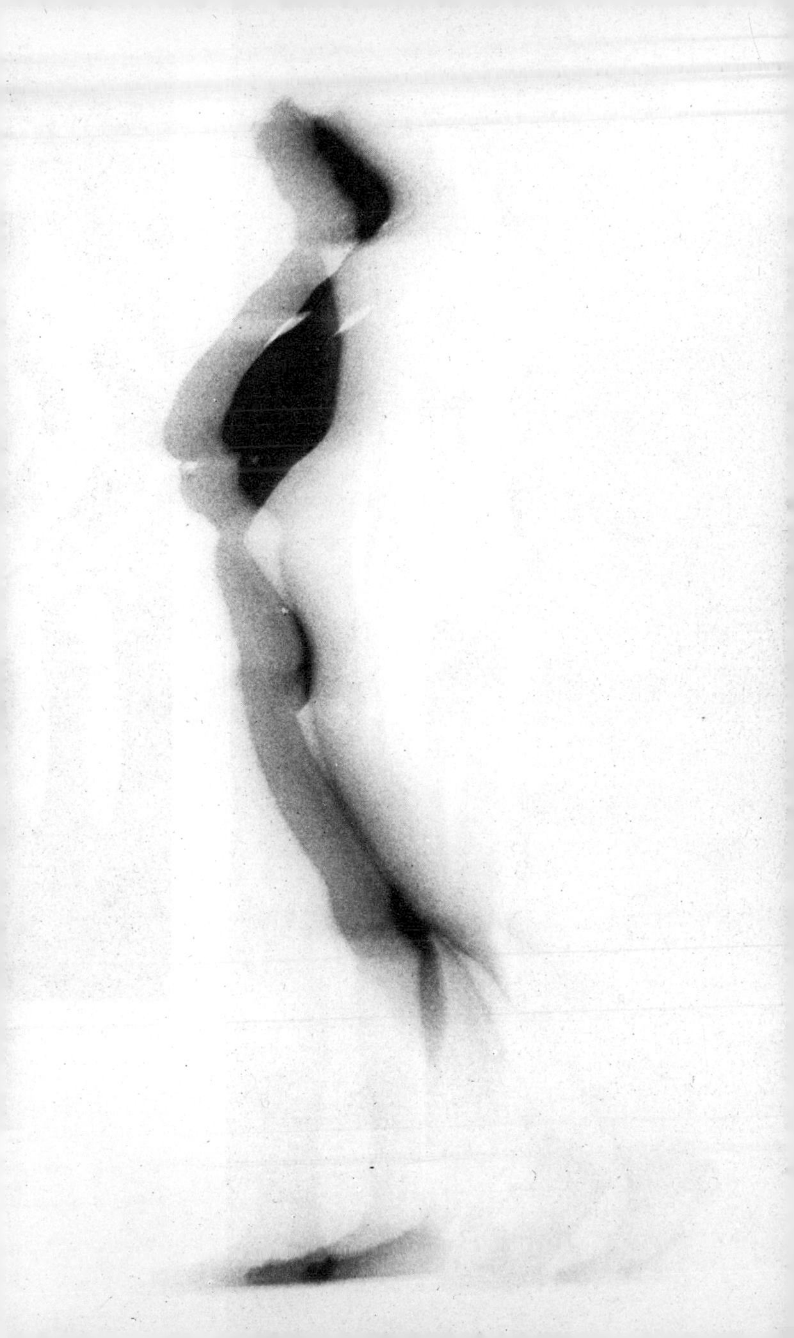

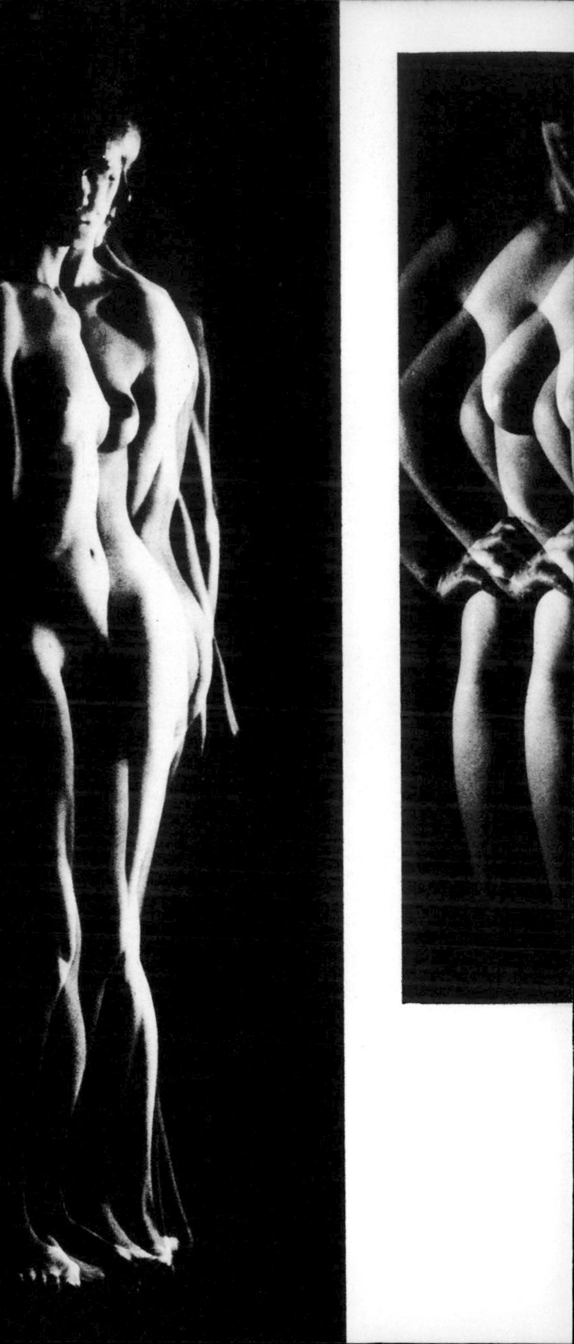

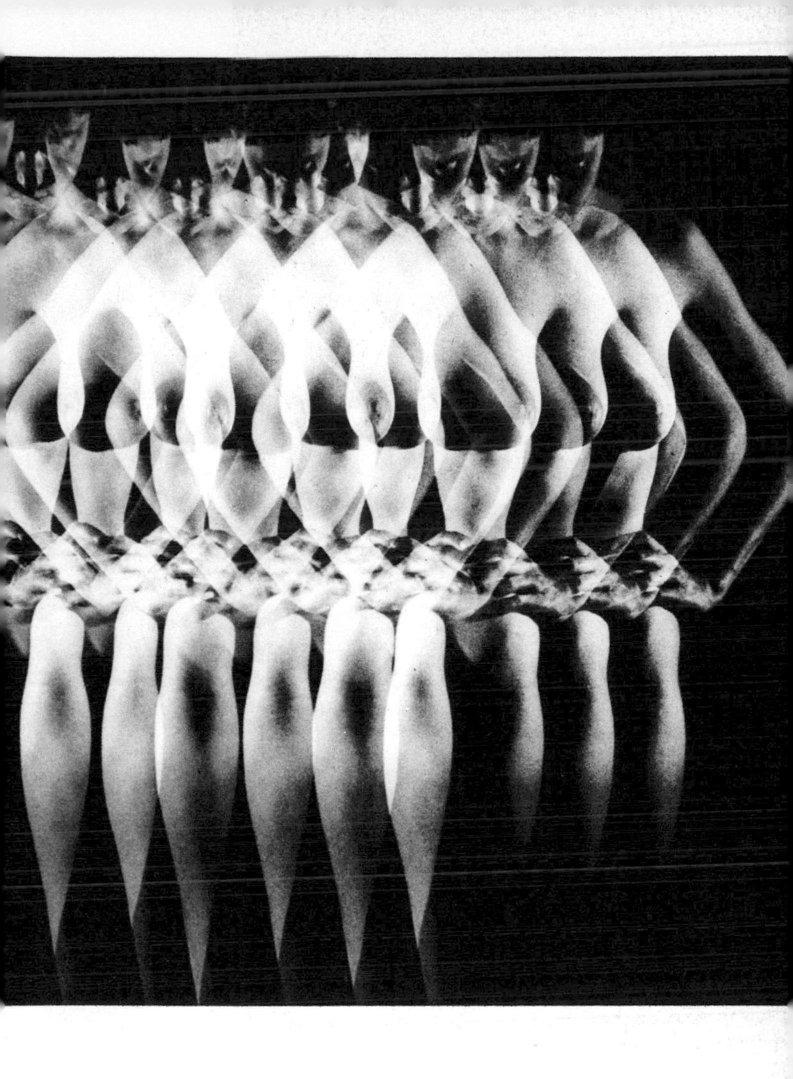

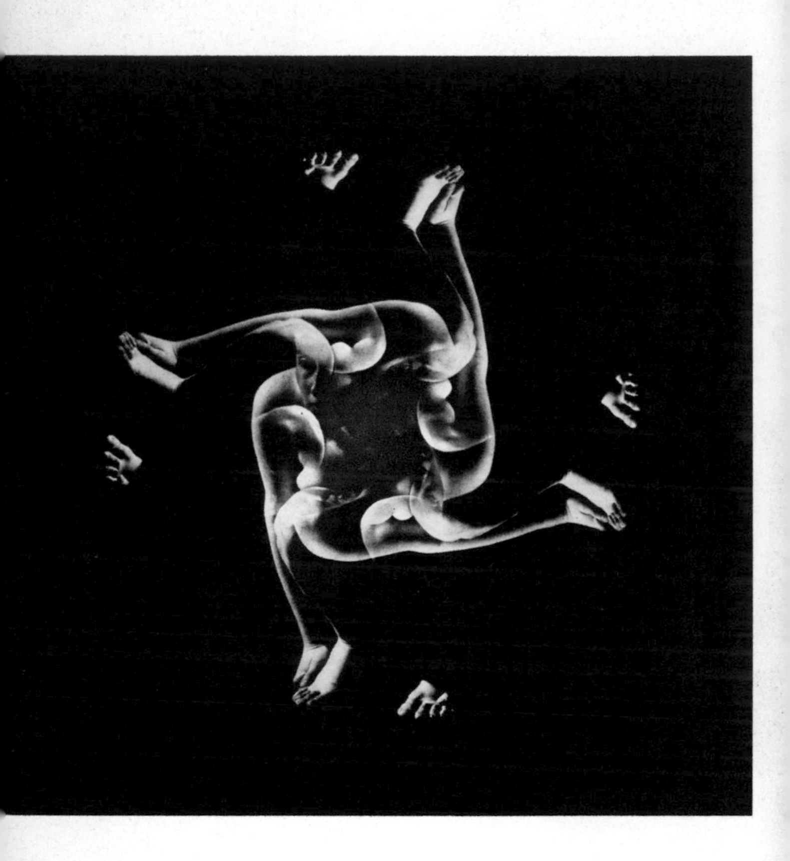

MARVIN NEWMAN

From the earliest photography of the nude to the present, the subject has usually been posed or at least directed in her movements by the photographer. The photojournalist of today—the kind of photographer who finds rather than creates his pictures—rarely photographs the nude, for the obvious reason that she is not often found in public. When she does occur, as in a burlesque theater, it requires some skill to photographically distill beauty from vulgarity and form from bumping, grinding movement. Marvin Newman has performed such a feat in these pictures. He has concentrated on the dancer herself and her complete absorption in her role. In her moving form we see again the models of Muybridge. The photos are also reminiscent of the softly focused dancing nudes photographed by Arnold Genthe some fifty years ago.

Photojournalism is a kind of reporting and its finest practitioners are good reporters. The mood and significance of these photographs are best described by Newman himself: "When I took these pictures on a winter night in Kansas City, theater burlesque was dying. The house was a third full, all down front. There was no chorus line, only a progression of house strippers, a headliner from out of town, and two old-time comics playing the old dirty jokes on each other. The orchestra was three pieces led by a matronly piano player with pince-nez and print dress, who looked as though she should have been home in her parlor on the farm playing love's old sweet songs and humming to herself. The strippers complained they couldn't bump and grind properly because the trumpet player, an old man who blew false notes, didn't have it. The theater was more than sixty years old. Someone told me that in a better time it had been an opera house. It did have a certain high opulence and elegance, but now dust and disrepair made it shabby and seedy. In this wretched setting, the stripper created beauty of a kind. As the lights progressively dimmed to that last soft, strange, blue light that approaches moonlight, the place and the girl became unreal, ephemeral. The stripper became hidden in that peculiar and private half-light; she became whatever you wanted her to be. The dreary stage with its musty hangings seemed to dissolve. The uncertain music was forgotten. The photographs were taken at this illusory moment. The vulgarity and sensuality of stripteasing became muted and ambiguous. Sex was made more real by being less real—by being half-spoken, half-shown, an implication, and the promise of the dream."

BILL BRANDT

Bill Brandt's discovery of the nude began with the purchase of an ancient Kodak pinhole camera. This polished mahogany antique had been used by Scotland Yard for the reproduction of police records. When Brandt, the best English photographer of this century, found the camera, it reposed in a Covent Garden secondhand store, its shutterless wide-angle lens permanently focused on infinity. Its archaic construction would seem intolerably limiting to most modern photographers, but it was precisely what Brandt wanted. He has expressed the belief that the technical development of photography has been so rapid that photographers have had little opportunity or desire to fully explore the potentialities of their medium. Brandt, a master craftsman, had grown tired of modern cameras that seemed to mimic human sight. He wanted to record the unstereotyped vision of a less conventional eye, and the old camera suited his need perfectly. The subject of the nude had fascinated him for some time and to it he brought the mysterious potentialities of the Kodak. The results were momentous.

Brandt has long been known for his sensitive photoreportage of the English scene and the haunting surreality of many of his pictures. In the case of these nudes, he was capable of learning what his camera could teach him. Though each of the photographs in the nude series is important in itself, their chronological progression graphically demonstrates Brandt's increasing insight and mastery of the camera. The surrealistic nudes of the interiors with their surprisingly undisturbing distortion of perspective are succeeded by the monumentally observed semi-abstract nudes of the seashore. These last pictures, with their beautifully simple forms, are reminiscent of the affinitive forms of Weston. Yet they differ from Weston in their stark transitions from white to black. They also markedly resemble sculpture, particularly the work of Brandt's fellow Englishman, Henry Moore. Despite these resemblances, however, all of Brandt's work is a uniquely powerful photographic statement about the nude, as well as a triumph of photographic technique.

When Brandt began to work with his camera, he was never quite sure what his picture would look like: he was forced to use long exposures and he could never exactly repeat a pose. The slightest movement of model or camera would bring about a completely different picture. Eventually, however, Brandt began to form a thorough conception of the camera's possibilities and, through it, of the possibilities of the nude.

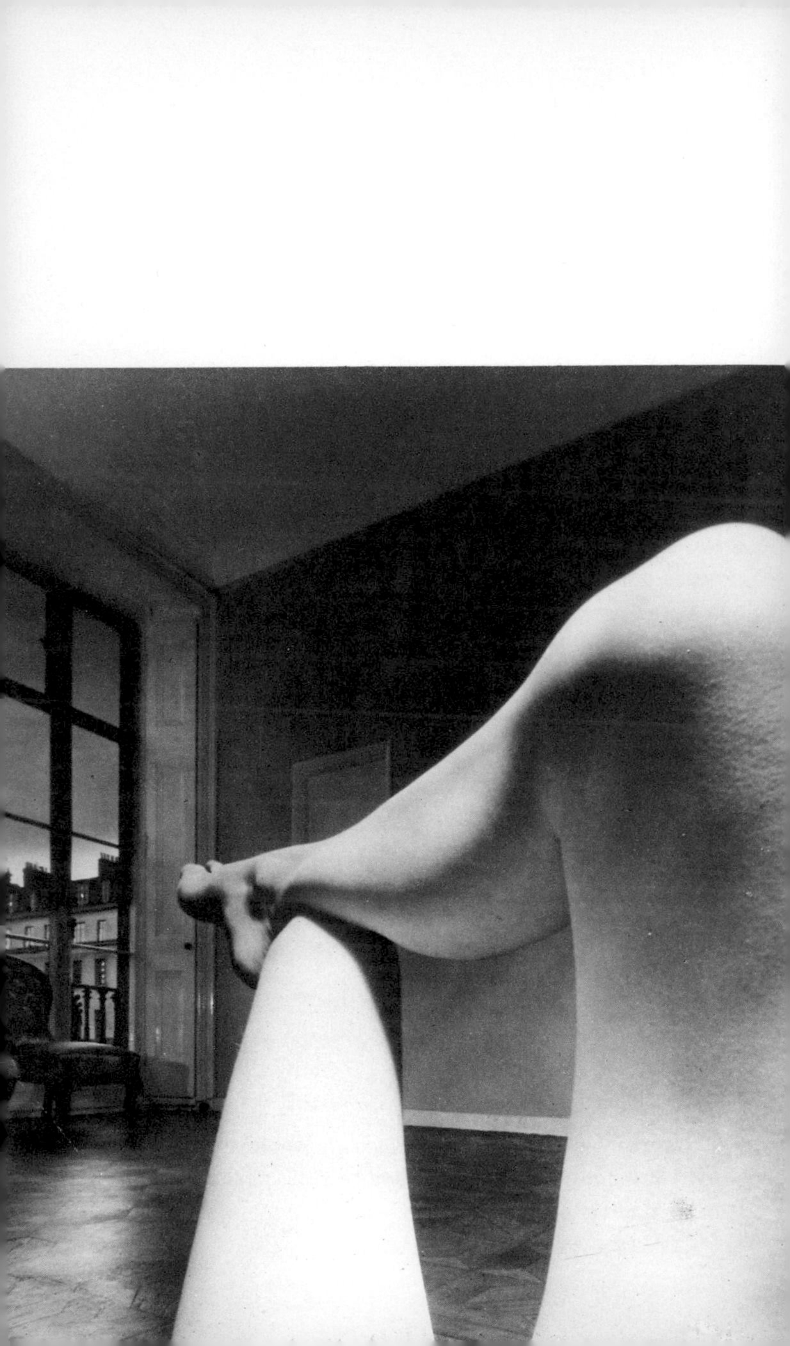

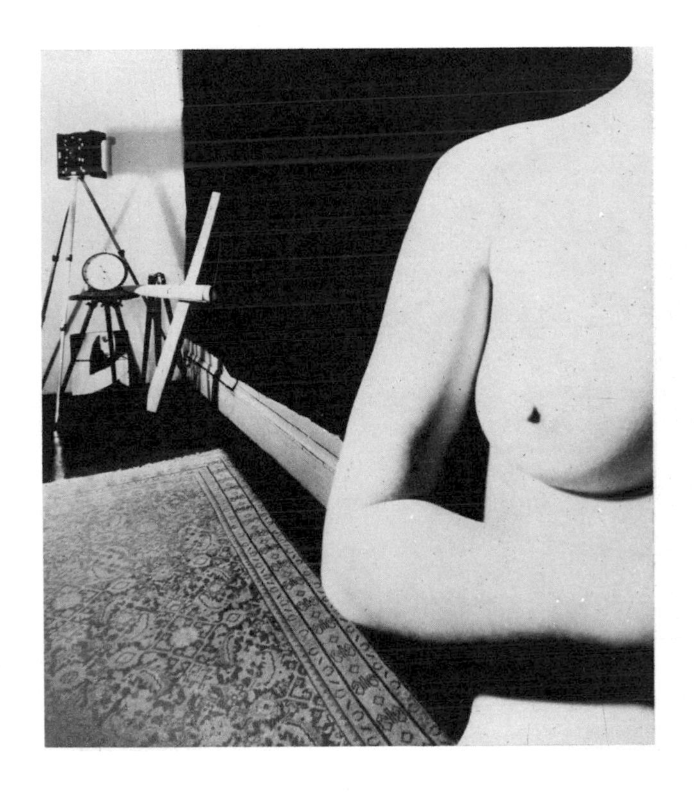

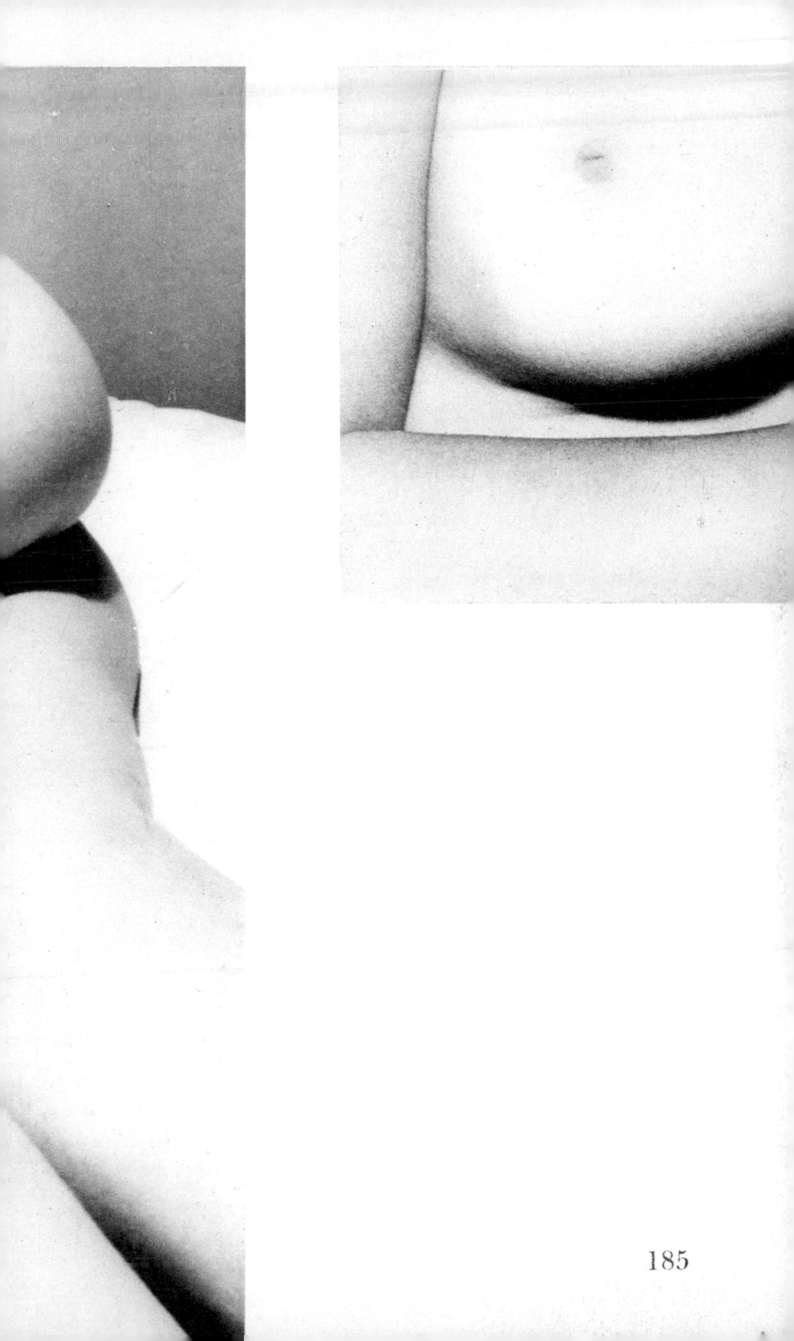

FRANK HORVAT

The nude is Mlle. Loulou Santiago. The setting is the Crazy Horse Saloon in Paris. Here the ingenious French have adapted and elaborated an American invention into forms weird and spectacular. "Le Strip-Tease" has become a Parisian institution, and practitioners like Mlle. Loulou have raised it to a kind of art. In these pictures by the French photographer Frank Horvat, Loulou is performing in the almost-nude, illuminated by a light projected through Spanish lace. The result is notable, and Horvat's photographs successfully impart the novelty and intensity of the girl's performance. And why not? As we have seen elsewhere, the beauty of the nude is not found only in the studio and poses. It can be found in reality, whether romantic (pages 139-147) or raucous (pages 169-175). Horvat, accomplished and versatile, is known for his work as a photo-journalist and as a fashion photographer. In his book J'Aime le Strip-Tease (for which these photographs were taken) he has explored the world of the Parisian strip clubs with the eye of a reporter and a sense for beauty, wherever it may be found. The effect of these photographs is erotic but never lewd—it can even be beautiful (pages 196-197). The girl is utterly absorbed in her performance. It is worth comparing these pictures with those of the American striptease by Marvin Newman. Both photographers have captured the essential sexuality of the performances and in their choice of mood and gesture have revealed the difference between the two approaches to the striptease: the overt and sweaty excitement of the American and the comparatively measured, dramatic eroticism of the French.

These photographs, taken in a darkened nightclub, also demonstrate the way in which photographers have exploited the increasing versatility of the camera. New vistas have been imaginatively explored, and the essential nude has been discovered in such dim and unlikely places as the Crazy Horse Saloon. There she occasionally emerges (as in these pictures) from a naked chorus and displays herself to the sensitive eye: beauty, universal but not anonymous; form, individual but not particular; mood evocative but not insistent. It is these qualities which have always distinguished the best photographic nudes from the merely pictorial or illustrative. This same arabesqued Loulou photographed by a lesser photographer would still be interesting because of her novelty. Through the keen eye of Frank Horvat she has become significant as well in her beauty of form and intensity of concentration in her performance.

J. FREDERICK SMITH

The photographed nude has by now become a familiar feature of advertising and illustration. In the work of the more accomplished photographers in these fields she can achieve a high quality of expression. Here, mood and nuance are all. Form is expressive rather than fundamental. Femininity is the key, as these pictures are often created for women. In other words, the quality rather than the substance of woman is stressed. The slim "figure" model is currently ideal for this kind of photograph because her figure, while feminine, is not too emphatically female. Her form, if not her sex, is invariably understated.

One of the most successful photographers in this genre is J. Frederick Smith of New York. His photographs reveal an idealized and romanticized nude. Her reveries take place in the most delicate surroundings; nature is tamed by her presence. This effect is not an easy thing for a photographer to achieve. He must tread a narrow path between the banal and the insipid. Smith accomplishes the task almost faultlessly. His nudes have charm and beauty and are grateful to be portrayed so. Femininity is not the least of woman's qualities.

Smith's ability to distill femininity is partially due to his train-

ing as an artist. Before becoming a professional photographer, he had established a reputation as a commercial artist and illustrator for leading magazines. In this latter role he often illustrated romantic fiction. Smith became interested in photography as a medium of expression when he began to use the camera to record models and backgrounds for story situations he was to illustrate. As a careful artist, his method of working is precise and considered. He photographically observes the model as she expresses herself within the context he has created for her. By careful selection of model and setting the desired effect is achieved. The method is almost that of the drama, with the photographer cast in the role of director. Though this method seems at first glance far removed from the methods of such photographers of the nude as Edward Weston and Bill Brandt, it is actually similar in one important respect: the nude is carefully observed for revelations of form, gesture, and mood. Where these photographers part company is in their individual conceptions of what is most significant in their vision. To Smith, the nude is the essence of femininity. To the others, an essential form or mysterious symbol. Her variety is infinite. It is certain that photographers will continue to find in her a fascinating challenge.

ROBERT WILSON

This portfolio presents the work of a young American photographer who has revealed life as well as beauty with his camera. Robert Wilson was born in Scranton, Pennsylvania, in 1936. The son of an itinerant jazz musician, he is a self-taught photographer. Through his camera he has explored reality, especially the world of the Negro, as he has found it in the restless cities of New York and Chicago. He now lives and works in Chicago, where he records life in the streets and parks. Influenced by the clean forms of Edward Weston's photographs and the fluent linearity of Japanese art, Wilson has sought to create pictures of "dynamic simplicity." This quality is present in his reportage as well as his still-lifes. In the form of the nude he has found an ideal subject for his discipline.

Though most photographers attempt to portray the nude at one time or another, only a minority continue to explore the subject throughout their careers. To these photographers the form of the nude often becomes a challenge and reference by which to judge and develop their vision. The young photographer quickly finds that the nude presents unexpected problems of mood and meaning as well as of composition and texture. He discovers that his pictures of this subject demand at least as much of his personal feelings as of his personal way of seeing. The erotic content of the nude must be recognized and aesthetically reconciled. The photographer must also force himself to see through eyes clear of narrow conceptions of beauty, for we wish to know the nude in all of her manifestations and nuances. It remains for photographers like Robert Wilson and his contemporaries to reveal their discoveries to us. Photographic revelations of the nude will never be exhausted as long as both photographers and their audience are determined to find the meaning of the nude wherever and however she may manifest herself.

In these photographs of Robert Wilson we also see the continuing influence of Edward Weston's nudes. But Wilson has made the pictures distinctively his own by his choice of lighting and composition. His approach to the model is more sympathetic and less analytical than Weston's: form and linearity are portrayed not for their own sakes, but as components of an individually beautiful woman. A comparison of these pictures with the work of Charles Swedlund, another younger photographer, affirms that the nude is still tirelessly revealing herself in new ways to new eyes.

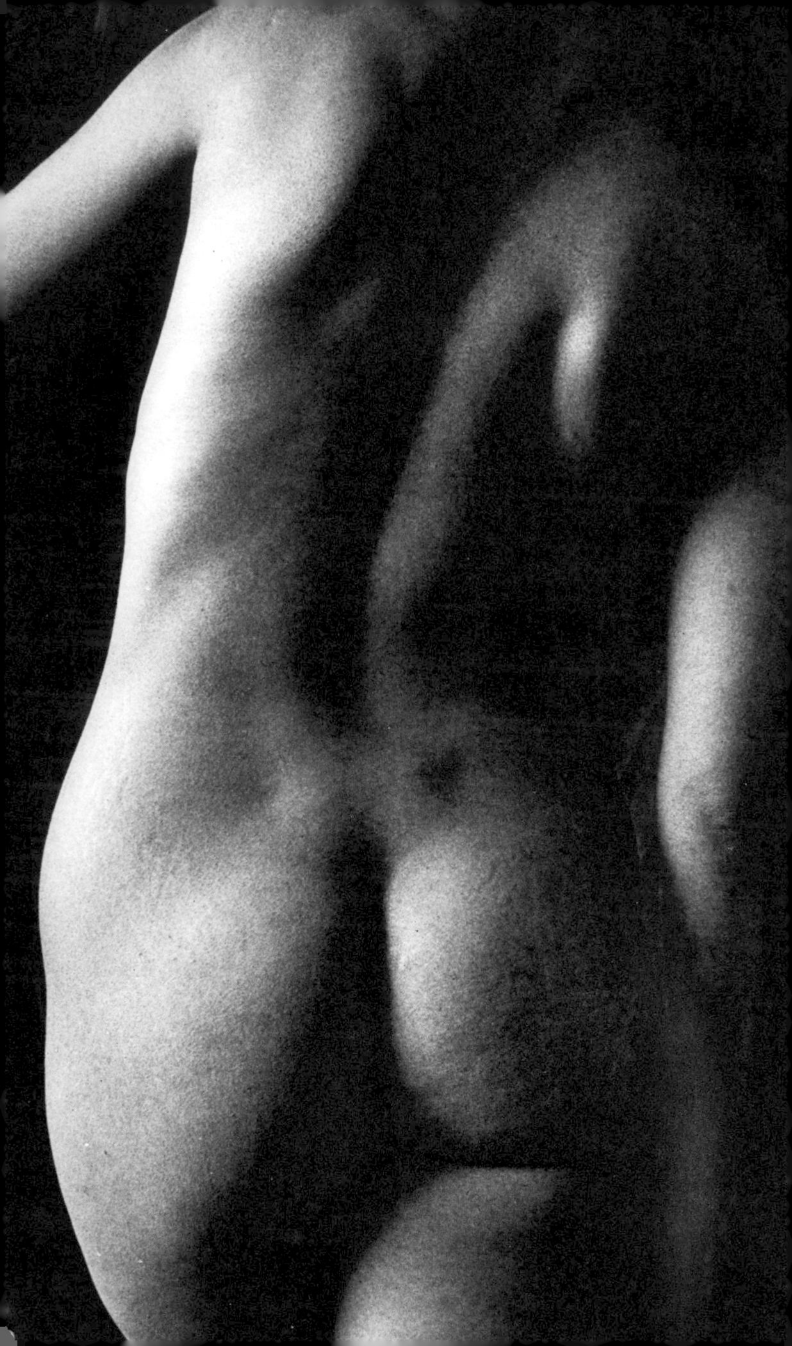

acknowledgments

The fascinating history of the nude in photography has, surprisingly, never before been the subject of a book. There have been brief surveys within the pages of photographic magazines or annuals, but no comprehensive, book-length treatment has been attempted. Yet there has long been need for such an assemblage as this book presents. This need is particularly acute today when we are being inundated with a flood of pin-up photography that obscures the significant pictures that have been (and are being) made of the nude. It must be emphasized, though, that this volume is not presented as a definitive collection of all of the significant work done with this subject. Certain names are conspicuous by their absence. Their exclusion is not due to oversight but to technicalities that could not be resolved.

Despite these omissions, it is hoped that this book will prove useful. The best photographs of the nude have too long been scattered in various publications and museum collections; some of these photographs have been almost inaccessible, many have never before been published.

The work of collecting and organizing the pictures was made possible by the friendly cooperation of all of the living photographers represented. The author is grateful for their enthusiastic interest in the project. Others whose information and suggestions were of great help are Grace Mayer of the Museum of Modern Art, New York, Hugh Edwards of the Art Institute of Chicago, Beaumont Newhall of George Eastman House, Rochester, and L. Wilson Kidd, Jr., of Washington, D. C. Much of the historical matter in the book was derived from Helmut Gernsheim's two important studies: THE HISTORY OF PHOTOGRAPHY (London, 1955) and CREATIVE PHOTOGRAPHY (London, 1962). Many of the photographs shown here first appeared in the pages of U. S. CAMERA ANNUAL, a publication that has consistently printed much of the significant photography of the nude done in the last few decades. Finally, the author must acknowledge the essential contribution of his co-editor Anthony LaRotonda in the selection of the photographs.